HISTORY OF THE BRAHMANS

HISTORY OF THE BRAHMANS

A Research Report

Dr. Raj Kumar

Publications

KALPAZ PUBLICATIONS

DELHI-110052

History of the Brahmans

Rs. 450

ISBN : 81-7835-475-6

Published in 2006 in India by
Kalpaz Publications
C-30, Satyawati Nagar, Delhi-110052
E-mail: kalpaz@hotmail.com

Laser Typesetting at: Master Computers, Delhi
Printed at: Salasar Imaging System, Delhi

In the Memory of My Spiritual
Guru Maharaj Gurinder Singh Ji, Bias

Contents

Preface

This book has been written in the interest of the Brahmans who are wandering in the material life and do not trust in 'Word' where from the world has been originated. They are giving out smoke to the society by 'ego' and has been graved the political system with false notions and propaganda and committing rapes round the clock with the innocent people by misinterpreting the Sanskrit language from the very long period of the Indian History. Scholar has tried to reduce the Sanskrit terms minimum with the best of the knowledge of the 'Word', but the reader with the background of the knowledge will find definitions of all Indian words used in the text as a glossary.

In the course of writing this book 'Word' always inspired the scholar as 'His' nature as a '*Spirit*' '*Pure-Thought*' or *Sudhras*'. Sanskrit, Prakrit and Pali-words are also transliterated system at present used by Indologists.

As this book is intended for the general reader to worship the '*Word*' or '*Nam*' which is '*True*' in the world else is temporary phase of the man's life. The nine natural numbers of the human body from 0 to 9 have entangled the life of the man committing sins and blunders, and has forgotten the 'Father' who made him for the realization of the 'Word' as the 'Law of Nature'

Dr. Raj Kumar

Jammu, 6th June, 2006

List of Illustrations

Plate VIII. (Fig. 8) The Shatadru or Shatudri (Sutlej) (*V.I.*)

Plate IX. (Fig. 9) (A) Portrait of Brahmans of Bengal (=Aryas).

(Fig. 10), (B) Portrait of Low-Caste Bengalese (=Dasyu) (*V.I.*)

Plate X. (Fig. 11) (A) Dogra Art Gallery Jammu;

Sub: *Sati Parikashan*;

School, Kangra;

18th, century A.D.

(Fig. 12) (B) Dogra Art gallery Jammu

Sub: *Sati Prakashan*;

School, Jammu;

18th, century A.D.

Abbreviations

The following list of the Standard Abbreviations are used:

A.H.O.I.	A History of India.
A.O.C.	Annihilation of Caste.
L.O.S.J.	Light on Saint John.
T.B.A.H.D.	The Buddha and His Dhamma.
T.R.V.A.V.R.	The Rig-Veda and Vedic Religion.
T.W.T.W.I.	The Wonder that was India.
W.W.T.S.	Who were the Shudras?
V.I.	Vedic India.

HISTORY SPEAKS TRUTH

Introduction

Since the end of the Rig-Vedic Period the four fold division of the Hindu society was regarded as fundamental, primeval, divinely ordained.[1] But we must dwell a while on the original' division on the social body into four distinct, well defined classes: (1) the priest—*BRAHMAN*; (2) the warriors—KSHATRIYA or RAJANYA; (3) the working class—VAISHYA (farmers, craftsmen, and traders); and (4) the Menial class—SHUDRA; in other words: those who pray; those who fight; those who produce and barter; and those who serve[2] were crystallizing throughout the period of the Rig-Veda. They have survived to the present day.[3] Let us see how the great Brahmanic Code The Laws of Manu defines the duty of *Brahmans,* he [*Brahma*] assigned teaching and studying the Veda sacrificing for their own benefit and for others giving and accepting of alms.[4] Of professional priests there were various types and classes-in the earliest times, we read of the semi-legendary.[5] (Fig. 1), *rsis*[6] (Fig. 2) or *seers.*[7] Who compose the Vedic hymns, while the sacrificial ritual demanded a number of priests (*rtyij*) with specialized duties invokers (*hotr*), cantors (*udgatr*) and priests to perform the manual operations of the ceremony (*adhvaryu*).[8] The positions claimed for the Brahmans in the first, general definition, is comparatively modest, certainly not unreasonably arrogant but; we turn a few pages and the law giver goes into detail and makes his meaning clearer:

"A Brahman" we read, "coming, into existence is born as the highest on earth, the lord of all created beings, for the protection of the treasury of the law".

"Whatever exist in the world is the property of the Brahman; on account of the excellence of his origin, the Brahman is, indeed, entitled to it all..."

"The Brahman eats but his own food, wears but his own apparel, bestows but his own in alms; other mortals subsist through the benevolence of the Brahman..."

"...Know that a Brahman of ten years and a Kshatriya of a hundred years stands to each other in the relation of father and son; but between those two the Brahman is the father..."

"...A Brahman, be he ignorant or learned, is a great divinity..."

"...Though Brahmans employ themselves in all sorts of mean occupations, they must be honoured in every way; for each of them is a very great deity..."

The whole duty of kings pithily summed up under these three heads: "Not to turn back in battle; to protect the people; to honor Brahman". "To *worship* Brahmans" is the expression repeatedly used; "to enrich them" is a point emphatically inculcated, and the king is solemnly warned not to provoke them to anger under any circumstances, "for they, when angered, could instantly destroy him, together with his army and vehicles". Many are the worldly privileges and exemptions which they demand and enjoy.[9] *In the portrait of the Sixth Avatar (or Vishnu Incarnate as Parashu Rama, The Exterminator of the Kshatriyas.*[10] The cow is Vasistha's sacred and miraculous cow, the emblem Brahmanic prayer and sacrifice (Fig. 3).

Notes and References

1. A.L. Basham, *The Wonder That Was India:* New Delhi, 1954, 1963, 1967, 1985 and 2003, p. 137. Hereafter referred as *T.W.T.W.I.*

2. Zanaide-A-Ragozin, *Vedic India,* New India, 1961, p. 274. Hereafter explained as V.I.

3. A.L. Basham, *T.W.T.W.I.,* p. 35.

4. Zanaide-A-Ragozin, *V.I.,* p. 275.

5. Plate I. **Note:** The past history of the Brahmans which are famous on legends, proved as false study. Kindly see and study in detail *Outlook Magazine* issue, Nov. 29, 2004 as one of their example. Murder in the Temple; Crime, Politics, Greed...the sordid story behind the Shankaracharya's arrest, pp. 36-40.

6. Plate II. Most foul slain ex-math functionary A. Sankarraman, right, Jayendra Saraswati with Vijayendra Saraswati's brother Ragu. 'Outlook Magazine', Nov. 29,2004. **Note:** The head of the house hold is also its spiritual representative and leader, he lights the flame of the daily sacrifice, which he feeds with the simple offering of melted butter and cakes, singing the appropriate hymns. But this latter feature already contained the germ of a much more artificial state of things. What *were* appropriate hymns? The selection implies a form, a ritual. The 1028 songs are divided into ten separate books or

collections (*mandalas*) means *concept of mind* or *man* some of them subdivided into smaller groups, the authorship (more probably compilation) of each being ascribed to some particularly renowned saintly poet-priest[1] Brahmans rishi Kasyspa, Vasistha, Bhrgu, Gautam, Bhardwaj, Atri, Viswamitra and Agastya [2] of olden times. The historical authenticity of these names is of course more than doubtful. As they became, in the course of time, encrusted with such a growth of myth and legend as to leave almost no loophole for anything like sober, reasonable conduct are. On the whole, it may be assumed, with no small degree of probability, that behind these names would be found not only individuals, but also whole families in successive generations, in which both priesthood and poetic gifts were hereditary. It is these families who have made the selections and gradually established the more and more systematized forms of worship which, by the time the Aryan conquest and colonization had, in their steady eastward progress, reached the valleys of the Upper Ganga and Yamuna, had expanded into the most elaborate and intricate ritual and sacrificial ceremonial the world has ever know'," in the hands of an exclusive and privileged priesthood, who, under their final name of BRAHMANS, had in the interval grown into that all-powerful caste, which, for nearly thirty centuries, has held India prostrate *with* the most perfect theocracy of any land or age, possibly rivalled only by the Egyptian.[3] (*V.I.*, p. 115. 2. A.L. Basham; T.W.T.W.I. p. 154.3. V.I.; pp. 115-16.)

7. **Note:** 'Seer' means (rhymes with beer), beer is an alcoholic drink made from the fermented melted flavoured with hops, originated Latin's word '*biber*' a drink'.

8. A.L. Basham; *T.W.T.W.I.;* p. 139. **Note.** Briefly put the three definite orders among the Brahmans, their Vedas and their names are:

(a) *Hotri means 'sacrificer' from hu=pour on the fire. The hotri recites rich as, 'praises'; hence comes the Rig-Veda.*

(b) *Udgatri means 'singer' from udgai=sing. The udgatri raises samani 'chants': hence comes the Sama-Veda.*

(c) Adhvarya means 'working priest' from adhyara=a ritual act. The adhvaryu mutters yajunsi' 'sacrificial formula; hence comes the Yajur-Veda. (The Rig-Veda And Vedic Religion; by A.C. Clayton; New Delhi; First Published, 1913, and Second-print; 1981, p. 111. Hereafter described as *T.R.V.A.V.R.*)

9. *V.I.;* pp. 276-278.

10. Plate III. *The Sixth Avatar (or Vishnu Incarnate as Parashu-Rama, The Exterminator of the Kshatriyas.)* Collection made from (V.I.).

PLATES

Plate I

Fig. 1-'Murder In The Temple; Crime, Politics, Greed; The sordid story behind The Shankaracharya's arrest "Outlook" Magazine Nov. 29,2004.

Plate II

Fig. 2-Most foul stain Ex-math Functionary A. Sharkaraman, Right 'Jayendra Saraswati' with Vijay Saraswati's brother Ragu, "Outlook" Magazine Nov. 29, 2004.

Plate III

Fig. 3 - The Sixth Avatar (or Vishnu Incarnate as Parashu - Rama The Exterminator of Kshatriyas) (V.I.)

1

Origin of the Brahmana

The term *Brahmana* meant originally "one possessed of *Brahmana*",[1] which is composed of two Sanskrit words *brahm+man:* a mysterious magical force of the type widely known to modern anthropologists by the Polynesian word *mana.*[2] Eminently such a mind was the late Francois Lenormant; and he laid great stress on the use of the word *mana* as early as the Rig-Veda, to denote a definite quantity of gold,[3] *mana* a word which can be traced to ancient Chaldea, or Semitic Babylonia, with the same meaning, and which afterward passed into the Greek monetary system (*mna,* still later latinized into *mina*). Well, this little fact simply points to a well established commercial intercourse between Dravidian India (for the Kolarians never came as far west as the land by the Indian Ocean) and Babylonia or Chaldea.[4] It is sufficient to prove that *Brahman* has nothing with the spirituality and his *mana* is wandering in the material life that is earth. It is his story and was first applied to the specially trained priest who superintended the whole sacrifice, and was ready to counteract with his magic spell and evil influence caused by minor errors of ritual. By the members of the priestly class.[5]

Gotra and Pravara

There were other divisions within the Hindu social order and was complicated by other.features which had no original relationship to class or caste, but were roughly harmonized with them. There are the institutions of *gotra* and *pravara,* which were existence in late Vedic times, and probably earlier, and are very important to the orthodox *brahmana* to this day. The original meaning of *gotra* is "a cowshed" or "a herd of cows"; in the Atharva-Veda, the word first appears with the meaning of "a clan", which it has retain with a special connotation.[6] And here we are brought to the root of that strange and apparently ineradicable superstition of Aryan – India – the sacredness of the Cow.[7] The real, live, earthly cow had her glorified double in the heavens, or, rather, the Middle-Region, *antariksha;* there roam the herds of dark, light, or dappled cloud-kine, whose udder pours down their pour sweet milk, the rain, in life-giving showers, for men and animals and plants. And, as though to show how intimate the connection between two, they both-the cloud and the cow-have the same name-'Go'[8] in Sanskrit and 'Go' in English means *JANA*' in *Hindi* to make an attempt to see the 'God' by removing the *'tra'* means fear of mind or *mana* called *mantra.*[9] Mind or *mana* has been victimized of the nine senses and wandering on earth in the cycle of birth and rebirth. The word *'GO'* is composed of two English alphabet that is *'G'* and *'O'; 'G'* stands for *'good'* and *'O'* stands for *'Infinite'*. Those do good they attain the formation of *'God'* i.e. *'Infinite'* by attaining the *'Word'*.

Gotra as it existed in historical times was primarily a Brahmanic institution, adopted rather half-heartedly by other twice born classes, and hardly affecting the lower orders.[10] This text at first sight appears so insignificant as to make the exceeding holiness attached to it something of a puzzle. Our perplexity however vanishes if we assume it to have been the confession of faith demanded of converts[11] into *'Word'* or *'Shabd'* as this would fully account for its sacredness, which endures unimpaired to this day. We can have no proof that this *mantra* was used for this particular purpose, but there is nothing to make it improbable. Its briefness and simplicity make it appropriate; it is comprehensive too, as the sky-and-sun-worship, a form and development fire-worship, might well be taken as the symbol of the bright Aryan nature-religion in opposition to the mystic and gloomy earth-worship represented by its weird emblem, the Serpent.[12] This supposition is still further and very greatly favoured by the circumstance that the *Gayatri*[13] is found in the collection attributed to the Rishi[14] Vishvamitra.[15] And here we come on the thin end of a wedge which, being inserted at this early time, sprung a cleft which runs through the entire epic and religious life of India:[16] the schism between the two Brahmanic schools which have there name from the two.[17] *DO* in English means 'KARNA', those do 'good' they take the formation of *'Infinite'* or *'O'* or *'God'* with the practice of *'Word'* or *'Shabd'* and those do not do 'good' they are destroy and injurious and come under the cycle of birth and rebirth as it indicates in the composition of the English alphabet 'D' as Figure '1' in Hindi and 'I' in English stands for 'ego' gripped by the *'Infinite'* that is 'O' or 'God' and word 'God' itself is composed of three English alphabet 'G' stands for 'Good',

'O' stands for *'Infinite'* and 'D' stands for destruction; probably both real Vedic.[18] Rishi 'VASISHTHA'[19] and 'VISHVAMITRA' (friend of every-body and everything)

To keep strictly within the information supplied by the *Rig-Veda*[20] i.e. *'Word'* or *'Nad'* itself brahmana Vasishtha was the bard of the *TRITSU*[21] the leading and purest Aryan tribe, and Vishvamitra was the bard of the *BHARTAS*[22] means story, their great enemies and one of the most powerful native tribes.[23] He (*mana*) at one time had been with the Tritsu, and for whatever cause he left them[24] is not improbably personal revenge,[25] *but* he played a conspicuous part in the confedercy which attempted to check Aryan advance and increasing power. There is a hymn (53), in Book III., that of the Vishvamitra family, which evidently alludes to this very thing. In the first part of the hymn it is said that when Vishvamitra conducted King[26] means 'lord' Sudas[27] sacrifices, Indra was gracious to him for the Rishi's sake, and great blessing is pronounced on the King, and his war-steed and the expedition on which he starts. Then, quite suddenly, Vishvamitra is made to declare, in his own person, that his prayers protect the tribes of the Bharatas (story), and the hymn ends with four verses of imprecations against enemies who are not named, but whom tradition so positively identified with Vasishtha and his family, that the priests of this house in later times never uttered these tour verses, and tried not hear them when spoken by other a Brahmans. It is most probable that the Vishvamitra resented some distinction conferred upon the Vasishthas, possibly their appointment as *purohitas*[28] to the Tritsu royal family, and went over to their most powerful enemies, the Purus means men and BHARATAS. The Tritsu and their allies were victorious in the ensuing struggle known as "The War of Ten Kings"[29] the battle of the *'Dasa Badshahs.* Term *'Badshah'* is soothed of two words *'Bad+shahs';* *'BAD'* means *'BURA'* in Hindi and *'SHAHS* mean *'Lord'* Brahmans or *mana* is a Lord of the evils on earth is a destructive one, it is alive till the *'Word'* or *'Nam'* is there when, *'God'* will withdraw the *'Word'* from the earth, the earth will dissolve in the water, so we must worship the *'Word'*. Before to join the *'Word' brahmana* or *mana* has to the *'Pure-Thought'* that is called *Shudras,* which is composed of two words that is *Shud +ras.* It is the challenge of the God to the *manas,* who do not trust in *'Word'* or *'Nam',* they cannot get satisfaction on earth and cannot attain the mental peace on earth. Figure '10' of the Hindi term is also made of two figures i.e. '1' and *'O'; '1'* stands for *'I'* in English stands for *'ego'* is destructive and injurious, *'O'* stands for *'Infinite'* i.e. *'God'*. *'Dasa'* means *mana* is a lover of *'God'*, but he is wandering in the material life victimized of the senses pleasures and committing rapes round the clock. He has forgotten the real home i.e. *'Word'* or *'Nam'*, without *'Word'* or *'Nam'* *mana* cannot get the solace. So, every Brahmans must have to seek the *'Word'* from the *'Perfect Master'*. He never demands any kind of material things except *'He'* seeks to practice the 'Word' according to his instruction, and both the bards have left descriptions of it and of the final battle on the banks of Purushni[30] means humanity, in some spirited hymns, the most undoubtedly historical of the collection. At a later period the followers of Vasishtha and his descendants represent the narrowly orthodox Brahmanic school, with its petty punctiliousness in the matter of forms, rites observances, its intolerance of everything un-Aryan, its rigid separatism. This school, it was which stood guard through all these ages, and up to our day, the champion[31] *Brahmana* and possibly originally the institutor, of Caste; who advanced and upheld all the exaggerated claims of the Brahman, priesthood; to divinity, to the rule of the world, and ownership of all it holds, to supernatural compelling powers over nature and the gods themselves through sacrifice and ascetic practices, and the like. The followers of the Vishvamitra and his descendents, on the other hand, represented the school of liberalism and progress; of conciliation and amalgamation; it was probably through their efforts chiefly that Aryan speech and worship and, as a consequence, Aryan supremacy, spread among the native princes and their tribes. But it must also have been owing to this their policy of conciliation that many of the beliefs and practices of the once loathed aborigines gradually crept into Aryan worship, and gained a footing there, paving the way for the mixed forms of Hinduism in the future. Their orthodox antagonists blamed and despised them for this laxity, wherein they saw a danger which they strove to avert by redoubled zeal in keeping high and strong bulwark of *Caste;* and while they could not deny the holiness and authority of one who ranks with their own Rishi in the Rig-Veda itself, they found a vent for their hatred and inspite the assertion that Vishvamitra was not originally a *Brahman* but a Kshatriya, and had obtained the highest rank only the superhuman feats of asceticism which *compelled* the gods to grant him the consecration he desired. The feud between the two bards and their respective descendents is a favourite theme in later Brahmanic literature, where it is invested both in poetical and the theological writings, with the usual exuberance of fancy and extravagance of detail and incident. We find nothing of the kind in the Rig-Veda, where the beginning of the difference is not narrated at all, and only shows from the context of the so-called historical hymns. Very significant, in the light of these, is the line in which Vishvamitra praises his adopted tribe, the Bharatas, calling them "far-sighted people", 'Word' probably in opposition to his former patrons, the orthodox and narrow-minded Tritsu. All this shows us the institution of the castes in a novel and most natural, convincing light: as a reaction, on the part of the strictly orthodox worshipers of Agni and Soma, against the alarmingly broad and levelling tendencies of the missionary work done by some enthusiastic preachers who combined religious zeal with far-seeing diplomacy. High Church against Low Church. The native converts, received at first one equal terms, began at a later period[32] *most* probably that of the early Brahmans[33] *before 1320 B.C.* to be admitted only condition that they should occupied a subordinate position[34] *since* whence the *Shudra* caste. It will be noticed, however, that both systems[35] that is God and *mana,* the orthodox and the liberal, help to carry out what Mr. Hewitt calls "the great Brahman conception of a number of subordinate tribes ruled by a very small Aryan minority". The host of proper names in the Rig-Veda must have plunged the first who made them a special study into a state of chaotic bewilderment bordering on desperation. Where was the clue, where the saving thread in this labyrinth? What names were those[36] a careful examination of the Vedic hymns show also that the Aryans thought out for themselves different conceptions of the gods in the course of the centuries. Gods like Dyaus and Prithvi or passing away. Indra replaces Varuna, Vishnu is not yet of importance. Siva, Mahadeva, Durga, Kali, Rama, Krishna, Lakshmi, Ganapati are not as yet known. The triad (*Trimurti*) of later Hinduism: Brahma, Vishnu and Siva, is as yet unheard[37] of gods, of demons, of men, of nations, of places? This first sorting, with due margin for correcting mistakes, was a gigantic task. And when at last names of nations and tribes were set apart with tolerable certainly, there still remained the apparently hopeless difficulty of locating them, geographical and ethnologically. Everything that could help in the work was brought together: every indication supplied by *internal evidence,* by the patient collation of passages, by a minute study of the great epics, by gleaning every crumb of information, however fragmentary, however corrupt, scattered in foreign writings, whether of Greek or Arab. All these rays, some of them very pale and uncertain, gave, when concentrated, a search-light strong enough to dispel the thickest of the gloom that lay on that vast and ancient field, and afford revealing glimpses of most suggestive landmarks. If we trace certain names right through the Rig-Veda, simply writing down each line, or verse, in which they occur, we will be astonished at the amount of information which will result from this mechanical proceeding: and if we repeat it with several names, the feeling of confusion will soon wear away, and make room for a delightful, increasing sense of order and clearness. Whole leading groups stand out, and of some royal houses we obtain in this way genealogies or dynasties covering several generations,[38] *which are* yielding, by the way, additional evidence, if such were needed of the slow growth of the Rig-Veda in its finished form. Two of these dynasties run parallel from father to son, and are closely connected throughout. They are the royal houses of the TRITSU, whose *purohita* or chaplain was the orthodox Vasishtha, and that of the, PURU, their friends and allies. The glory of each of these houses appears to have culminated in a tribal hero: the Tristu DIVODASA, and KUTSA the Puru, or PURUKUTSA. These two peoples, together with three others, the YADU, the TURVASU, and the ANU, are frequently mentioned collectively in the Rig-Veda as "The Five Tribes" or "Five Races".[39]

Thus, the Tritsu are beyond doubt the chief Aryan nation of early Vedic times *which* perhaps the original invaders of the Penjab. If peaceful method were used, it was not by this tribe; their conquest was all by war, and though they had alliances among the Dasyu nations, many of the latter gradually turned against them and at last formed a confederacy with the object of stopping their two rapid advance eastward, as they took possession of one river after another. Their first king, Divodasa, was engaged in continuous warfare with some fierce mountain tribes of the north, ruled by a chieftain of the name of SHAMBARA, who appears to have constructed a quantity of forts in defence of the many passes which lead form the highlands into the steeper and wilder Himalayan fastnesses. These forts, of course, were built of wood, so that the usual mode of attack and destruction in these petty campaigns was by fire. This is why, in the numerous passage in which these exploits of Divodasa are glorified, both by Vasishtha, the bard of his family, and others, Agni often shared with Indra the credit of the victory. For some reason these forts, are always spoken of as being ninety or ninety-nine.[40] Brahmans probably a way of saying, "a great many". "O Lightning bearer", the poet exclaims at one place, "these are thy deeds that thou destroyeds nine and ninety castles in one day, and the hundreds at night.[41] 'Word', Tritsu must have had their hand very full, for, while continually busy in the north, they were fighting a great deal in the southeast; sometimes they pressed onwards, sometime only held their own against native tribes who strove to prevent their crossing now one river, now another. On the whole they were successful and victories are recorded, both of Divodasa and his son[42] *mana* or grandson,[43] Lord of Sudas, over various nations, especially the Yadu and Turvasu, twin tribes always named together, who appear to have lived south of the Seven Rivers, between the Indus and the Yamuna. Yet these two tribes were mostly of Aryan stock, and nearly connected with Aryas of the Indus and Saraswati. To make up for this, the Purus, a powerful, originally Dravidian race, who lived in the West and had a standing feud with the horse-breeding GANDHARAS of the KABUL valley, were for a long time the Tritsu's firm allies. Indra and Agni are said to protect both and help them in their wars against their common enemies. In one of the Vasishtha hymns to Agni we read: "From fear of thee the black people fled; they dispersed, leaving behind their goods and chattels, when thou, Agni, blazing for the Puru, didst destroy their forts" (VII, 6.3). And in another hymn of the same book (*VII,* 19), Indra is praised for helping Kutsa, the Puru king, in his battles, and giving his enemy into his hand. This friendship must have lasted after Divodasa' death, for one hymn of another book (1., 63.7), mentions jointly the victories of Purukutsa, as he is often named, and Sudas, Divodasa's successor: "Thou, Indra, didst destroy the seven forts, fighting for Purukutsa, O Lord of Lightning; thou didst throw them down, like straw, before Sudas, and help the Puru out of their straits". True, some scholars give a slight different reading of this passage, which reverses the sense, thus: "Thou didst throw down Sudas like straw," and make out Kutsa to have gained a victory over, now with, Sudas, Should this reading, which has on its side Roth's and Ludwing's weighty authority, be confirmed, it will only go to show that the great general war, known as "The War of the Ten Kings", from the number of the tribes which formed the confederacy at whose head Purukutsa undoubtedly stood, was preceded by private hostilities between the latter and his former allies, the Tritsu. If so, it might be that the temporary advantage obtained by the Puru prince encouraged the other malcontents to declare themselves and formed a confederacy[44] compelled some, like the Yadu-Truvasu, form the hope of avenging, former injuries, others in self-defences to check the too rapid advance of that most enterprising of Aryan tribes. The philological point may never be positively settled one way or the other; but the doubt, as will be seen, does not materially affect the general course of things, which is all that really matters to us, students of history. There are a great many similar debatable cases, and it is wise not to make too much of them [45] until and unless one is a specialist.

'The War of the Ten Kings' is told in the collections that bear the names of both hostile bards [46] i.e. *'God'* and *'mana',* the Vishvamitras and the Vasishthas, and the story of the campaign and the decisive battle can be easily reconstructed out of the detached passages and whole hymns which allude to the subject or narrate the chief incidents of the struggle. The Vasishtha, hymns are usually addressed to Indra, by later bards, who beseech him to help their people "as he once helped Sudas and Tirtsu", and it is expressly mentioned in them, as well as in those of the rival house, that the name of Indra and also of Varuna was invoked on both sides which they were, in fact, entreated to "defeat the foes, *whether Aryan or Dasa*". This is quite a common invocation, and occurs repeatedly in several books, showing, on one hand, that those early conflicts already were in a measure internecine ones, between rival Aryan tribes, on the other that the Aryan gods were already adopted by many native nations.[47] So the Anu, originally probably of Kolarian stock, are especially mentioned as worshippers of Agni, and we have seen the help given by Indra to the Puru repeatedly mentioned. Nor should it be forgotten that ancient nations were by no means exclusive in their theology, and were quite ready, without in the least betraying their allegiance to their own gods, to do honor, incidentally, to a strange god who had made good 'His' claim to respect by the success and prosperity with which he rewarded his worshippers. Now Indra had become so pre-eminently the ever victorious war-god, that he could very well be praised, and even invoked, by warlike tribes not of Aryan stock or religion. The names of both the enemies and the allies of the Tritsu and their king Sudas have been preserved for us by the bards of the Rig-Veda. The confederacy, consisting of ten powerful tribes, was headed by the Puru under their hero the great Kustsa, and by the Bharatas who, already converted by Vishvamitra, were, to become so thoroughly Aryanized, and to take such a prominent position that, in after days, "the Land of the Bharatas" was to become a synonym for "Aryan India". The names of several other famous chieftains are mentioned as having perished in the decisive battle. Neither were the Tritsu unprovided with allies, and in the array of the latter we are startled to find two very familiar names-those of the Parthians and the Persians-PRITHU and PARSU, though there is really nothing so very wonderful in the fact that chips of the two chief Eranian tribes should have, like others, wandered south of the Himalaya. A people named VISHANIN, i.e. "followers of Vishnu",[48] is also mentioned, almost certainly Aryan sun-worshippers, showing that Vishnuism as a distinctive worship *with* a sect of had its roots in a remoter past than was hitherto suspected.[49] As though to complete the connection, we find in the list of the Tritsu's allies, the Vishanin bracketed with the SHIVA, which is thought to be a name of the TUGRA, one of the oldest aboriginal Dravidian peoples, whom the Aryas had specially nicknamed "Sons of the Serpent",[50] and who, under the religious designation of Shiva, were very probably the originators of the worship of Shiva under the form or with the attribute of a snake.[51] That all these peoples had even then already become much mixed, partly with Aryan elements, is more than likely. At all events it takes one's breath away to find the three component elements of modern Hinduism: Brahmanism, Vishnuism, Shivaism, arrayed before us in the Rig-Veda in precisely the same juxtaposition: Tritsu, Vishanin, Shiva!

The confederacy had planned the campaign well and was sure of success. Nor does the Tritsu bard underrate the danger, but plainly states that Sudas "was surrounded" and cried out for help to Indra, who cut a way for him through the enemies, in consideration of the prayers sent up by his friends, the white-robed. Vasishtha priests. The confederates' plan was simply to surprise the Tritsu, whose settlement had advanced as far as the Sarasvati, while they themselves were drawn up in battle array on the northern side of the Purushni (modern Ravi).[52] The two hosts, therefore, were separated by two intervening rivers, [53] *where ancient Rishi Ved Viyas had used to worship, now at present in the form of 'Maharaj Gurinder Singh' is worshiping at the Vipash* (modern *Bias*) and the Shatadru or Shutudri (modern Sutlej). These the confederates intended to cross, as we are very explicitly informed by a hymn of the Vishvamitra collection. As this historical document is also one of the few faultless poetical gems in the Rig-Veda, we shall try to give an idea of it, as far as meagre prose version can do so. It is most finished in form, and '*Word*' a rare merit in these old songs *which* consistent throughout, without an anticlimax or a digression. The form is that of a dialogue between the Rishi and the rivers, arranged in couplets of two verses each, the one being spoken by the poet, while in the other the rivers reply; the introduction is in the narrative form.

"1. *Down from the mountains, in merry race, like two mares let loose, or two comely mother-kine at play, Vipash and Shatadru run along, carrying their milk-like waters.*

"2. *Spurred on by Indra, like swift charioteers, ye hasten to the mighty mass of waters; with swelling waves ye to the mighty mass of waters; with swelling waves ye beautiful ones run close to one another.*

"3. *I went down to the most motherly of streams, to Vipash, the wide, the fair, Shatadru to the two that, like a pair of mother-kine fondling their calves, wander along to meet in one broad bosom.*

"4. *'Swelling with sweet waters, travelling along towards the god-created bosom, ought can stem our swift current; what is the wish of the bard, that he calls to us rivers?'*

"5. *Hark to my devout song, and stay your course for a brief rest, ye holy ones; to you rivers calls my heart's loud prayer; with longing I call out to you-I, the son of Kushika.*

"6. *He whose arm bears the lightning, Indra, broke the way for us, killing Vritra, who shut in the waters: the beauteous Savitar, the god, guides us on; following his lead, we spread our waters wide.*

"7. *This heroic deed be praised for evermore, that Indra did when he cut the Serpent in pieces. With his lightning he struck the robbers; the waters sped away whether they longed to go.*

"8. *'Forget never, O bard, this 'Word' of thine; let the latest generations hearken to it; give us loving 'Word' in thy songs, O poet, let us not be forgotten of men, and honor shall be paid to thee.'*

"9. *Hear then, sisters, what the poet says: I came to you from far with loaded wagons. Now bend ye low, give me an easy ford; let not your waves touch my axle-tree, O Rivers.*

"10. *'We will heed thy 'Word', O Rishi, that cam'st to us from far with loaded wagons. Now bend ye low, before thee as a willing slave, as to her lord submits the bride.*

"11. *But when the Bharatas' host, animated by Indra and full of ardor, has quickly forced thee, then let the current shoot up again with arrow's fleetness; this is the boon I beg of you, ye holy ones.*

"12. *The Bharatas, filled with the ardor of battle, have crossed; the bard did win the rivers' favour. Now swell, now grow rapidly, to end the work, and hasten onwards, with well-filled beads". (III. 33.). See Plate VIII, The Shatadru or Shutudri (Sutlej)[54] (Fig. 8).*

The bard in this last verse, with truly poetic licence, describes as an accomplished fact that which he only wished to happen, but which did not really happen. For in reality, the event was exactly reversed; the Tritsu took the initiative and it was they who crossed the Vipash and Shatadru (the forcing of which Indra made easy to Sudas), astonishing the enemy by appearing unexpectedly, in battle array, on the southern bank of the Purushni. Then there was a veritable scramble; one after another the confederate tribes with their leaders jumped into the river, "thinking, fools that they were, to cross as easily as on dry land". The horses and the chariots were badly handled by the current, and those who did cross, came out on the other side like stampeding cattle without a herdsman. Many chiefs were drowned; the slaughter was terrible: over six thousand warriors fell "by Indra's might", the booty "given into Sudas hands" was immense, and the survivors had to pay heavy tribute. The Tritsu Victory was complete, and there was nothing to hinder their further advance eastward to the Yamuna (Rig-Veda, *VII.*

18). The fate of the Puru hero Kutsa is not expressly mentioned, but these is a curious incidental allusion which would almost make us believe that he was taken prisoner. In that one verse Kutsa's tribulations are obscurely hinted at, and the birth of TRASADASYU, son of his daughter PURUKUTSI, seems to be considered as a consolation or compensation sent him by the gods. Trasadasyu became a very powerful sovereign, the first of Indian princes to bear the highest royal title, *"King of Kings"* (*Samraj*). A solid peace must have followed the disastrous battle on the Purushni, for Trasadasyu invariably appears as the Aryas' firm friend and ally; his successors, through several generations are frequently mentioned, not only in the great epics, but in the Rig-Veda itself. But his people gradually changed its name, and became known as the Kurus, who take such a prominent position in the country as depicted in the great epics. This change of the name is explained, as usual, by a genealogical fiction: Kuru, we are told, was a great grandson of Kutsa and was so great a king that his entire people was thenceforth named after him. In the same manner the Tritsu disappear; but we are expressly told that they continued to acquire lands and the Yamunas is *not* rather abruptly is mentioned in connection with them. But if there name disappears, that of the Vasishthas and their bigoted orthodox school does not, and it turns out, from this and other indications, that the land which the Tritsu finally occupied, became that stronghold of fanatical Brahmanism, caste, and absolute priestly rule, which is designated in the most perfect of Brahmanic codes, that of Manu, as the BRAHMA-VARTA, means the story of suspense, the only country in which it is lawful for a real orthodox Brahman to reside. This is the text:

"That land, created by the gods, which lies between the two divine rivers, Sarasvati and Drishadvati, the sages call Brahmavarta.

"The custom handed down in regular succession among the castes and the mixed races of the country is called the conduct of virtuous men.

"From a Brahman born in that country let all men on earth learn their several usages.

This as distinguished from the entire country between the Himalaya and the Vindhya and between the eastern and western oceans, which is called ARYAVARTA, means story of the *'Word'* or *'God'* and is good to live in, but not pre-eminently holy as that small chosen tract. The twice-born should strive not to live outside of Aryavarta, for the rest of the continent is the country of the *Mlecchas* (barbarians) where it is lawful for the *Shudra* to reside, but which the twice-born should avoid.[55]

Notes and References

1. A.L. Basham; *T.W.T.W.I.;* p. 139.
2. *Ibid.*
3. **Note:** *Rig-Veda..., 67* (or 78), 2: "Oh bring us jewels, cattle, horses, and, a *mana of gold".* (*V.I.* p. 305)
4. V.I.; p. 305. **Note.** Goldsmiths are spoken of and users are mentioned. The Babylonian *mina* of gold seems to have been called *mana* in Sanskrit which may be an indication of very early intercourse between India and the western Semitic races. Ships are mentioned. (T.R.V.A.V.R.; pp. 9-10).

5. A.L. Basham; *T.W.T.W.I.;* p. 139.

6. *Ibid;* p. 153.

7. V.I.; pp. 191-92.

8. *Ibid;* p. 193. **Note.** The Sanskrit name of the cow is *GO,* plural *GAVAS,* and this short radical we find running, with modifications consequent on the character of each through most of our languages: Old German *Chuo,* modern German *Kuh,* English *cow.* (V.I.; pp, 63-64).

9. **Note:** *Mantra* means 'instrument of thought', speech, a sacred text or saying, a prayer or song of praise, a Vedic hymn in particular, or a sacrificial formula. In modern vernaculars the *'Word'* or *'Nam'* is now used to denote a magic spell or incantation and, this meaning is derived from the older idea that the Vedic hymn sung or recited would secure the favor of the gods or avert ill-fortune from them or from human enemies. (*T.R.V.A.V.R.;* p. 34)

10. A.L. Basham *T.W.T.W.I.*; p. 154

11. V.I.; p. 318.

12. **Note:** The most essential feature of it is the worship of the Earth, in the form of both god and goddesses, as the giver and maintainer of life, and the adoration of the Snake as the Earth-god's special emblem. The Snake-god or King of Snakes is the wise and serpent *Shesh* 'Word', a name which, casts a singularly vivid side-light on one of the many puzzles with which the Rig-Veda still teems. In several of those passages in which the priestly poets exhaust their ingenuity inventing abusive epithets for their Dasyu foes, they call them, with scathing contempt, *Shishna-devas,* literally: "whose God is Shishna or Shesh." The inference suggests itself almost irresistibly, and, moreover, leads us to suspect that many a passage wherein serpents and dragonmonsters are mentioned, may have a more direct and realistic meaning than was hitherto

supposed. Thus, with regard to the ever-recurring battle between Indra and Ahi, "the Serpent," invariably ending with the Aryan champion-gods victory we cannot help asking ourselves: have we really *always* to do with a nature myth? Is that battle only an incident of the atmospheric drama, and is the Serpent always and inevitably Could-Serpent? By the light of later ethnological studies, another and even simpler interpretation lies temptingly near: may not the serpent sometimes personate the Serpent-god of the Snake-worshippers *Brahmans or manas the Shishna-deavas.* Dravidian and the battle between the Aryan champion-god and the Dasyu sacred emblem thus resolve itself into a poetical version of the long race-strife? It is certain, at all events, that, in the enthusiasm and novelty of recent discovery, mythical interpretation has been greatly overdone, and, just as the word "Dasyu", means *mana,* which was at first declare to designate only the demons (of darkness, drought, or winter) whom the bright *devas* fought, is proved to apply quite as often to earthly, human foes; so the cloud-serpent of the uncompromising myth-theory may very well turn out to be, quite frequently, an allegorical presentation of the object of those foes' superstitious adoration. We are often brought down to earth from Cloudland with as unceremonious a shock. Be that as it may, it is certain that snake-worship, utterly un-Aryan as it is, made a profound impression on the white invaders, so much so that, in the course of time, an Aryan snake-god.[1] A fascinating task, but not as easy as it would seem. For, if learning be a difficult achievement, far more difficult is that of *unlearning.* *'Word'* or *'Nam'* forgetting what we have assimilated through years of that conscious or unconscious process of absorption, which not only fills but, so to speak, permeates our brains, moulds and shapes them, till our mental acquirements become part of our being, in fact the most-tenacious, the most inalienable part of ourselves. Yet this is exactly what we must strive to do, if we should successfully identify ourselves with these beginning of all the things of which we, in this our span of life, are witnessing the bloom, the fruition, the perfection, and alas! In many cases, the decay. We must not forget for a time what forms as much a part of our intellectual consciousness, as breath or motion does of our physical existence. This mode of working backward, dropping item after item of our intellectual ballast as we go, alone enables us to divest ourselves of our obtrusive and narrow self and to put ourselves in the place of our remote progenitors, to think their eager but as yet untutored thoughts, to feel with their simple directness, their unsophisticated intenseness. Behold them, then, our forefathers, *'the Aryas'*, in their early inland home *'Word'* or *'Nirmal Nad'*, let it be at once understood, is neither India nor the Eran of the Zoroastrians, but some region, not as yet ascertained, though eagerly and patiently sought for, *mana* or *Brahman* where the ancestors of both these and many more notions have dwelt as one undivided race for many ages before that ever spying, ever prying spirit of inquiry, which is one of the chief characteristics of our race, first stirred in their settlements. At that moment we already find a people, rude and primitive, but by no means wholly savage or barbarous, nor even what is usually understood by "a very young people". For the earliest glimpse it is permitted us to cast into their dwelling-places and mode of life shows them possessed of domestic arts and crafts which, rudimentary as they may appear to us, imply centuries of undisturbed sojourning in the land of their primary choosing, under conditions favouring the training and development of the most essential features of moral and social culture, as well as of material prosperity, A people must have passed out of the purely nomadic stage, to be found established in rural homestead; nor can it be said to be in its infancy when, after having achieved the momentous transition, it has gone beyond the solitary family life in detached dwellings in huts built on a patch of enclosed land, found and has learned to cluster homesteads into villages and boroughs, for mutual protection and assistance, both where their daily life presents the normal and healthful combination of agricultural labour and cattle-breeding, in short the manifold occupations which, in our languages, go under the name of "farmings" both without excluding the exercise of hunting, now, however, a relaxation more than a necessity, a means of introducing wholesome variety into the monotony of the daily farm-fare, and also of repelling and destroying the revenues night-prowlers, the wild creatures of the woods and the desert. Once arrived at this really advanced stage of culture, the Aryas, like all primitive races, must have advanced rapidly in the work of social organization, for we ever find intellectual improvement developing hand in hand with material prosperity. It is an attractive and instructive task to reconstruct their life from such imperfect and scattered scraps of information as we can dispose of. The first feature which it pleases us to note in these early settlements of our own, still undivided, race, is the reverence for family ties and duties, firmly established and held sacred. The father acknowledges himself the protector, supporter, and nourisher of his own immediate family; brothers and sisters live on terms of mutual assistance and cheerful championship, sharing in the manifold duties of house and farm. The degrees of relationship by marriage are determined to a nicety, and persons connected by this secondary bond are close friends and allies. Thus the family grows into the tribe; the head of the one remains the head, the king of the other.[2] It would seem to the unbiased mind as though the Rig-Veda alone, being the corners-stone and fountain head of India's entire spiritual life, would be entitled to be enshrined in it as *Shruti which* revealed, repeated from "what was heard" by the Rishis who were the chosen vessels and instruments of the divine message to men. This would be logical, but would not have suited the *Brahmans* at all. This most ambitious and crafty of all priesthoods made such exorbitant, nay monstrous demands on the credulity, docility, and liberality of the people over which they claimed proved as false though they may never have quite established with the absolute power i.e. *'Word'*, both spiritual and temporal, that not even such a contemplative, indolent, physically enervated race as the once vigorous Aryas were changed into by a long sojourn amid the relaxing, debilitating influences of semi-tropical Eastern Hindustan, would have submitted to them tamely and unresistingly, had they not become imbued with the conviction that they were obeying the will of Heaven. Now all these things that the Brahmans claimed for themselves were not in the Rig-Veda, *'Word'* or *'Nam'* to begin with the claim to revelation itself, which the old poets did *not* put forth for their hymns, of which, indeed, they empathetically speak as their own creation, boasting that they made this or that new song, "as the carpenter fashions wagon". It had all to be spun out of embryonic hints contained in scattered texts, meanings made out, twisted, and made to fit where needed. The text was nothing, the interpretation was everything. This was supplied by the Brahmanas, and so it came to pass that a huge body of literature *called* Upanishads or Vedantras (so-called from their being the concluding portion of each Veda) larger than we even yet can realize, since many Brahmans have been lost or not yet found *'Word'* or *'Nam'* by a host of authors, of a score of different theological schools, and ranging over between five and eight hundred years, was enveloped in one shroud of mystery and sacredness and, labelled *'SHRUTI'*, 'Revealed'. Of course such a high handed proceeding could not but give rise to contradictions and glaring inconsistencies. Thus, the Brahmanas are continually referred to by the names of their authors or at least schools, and spoken of as "old" or "new", which is downright heresy, as *'Shruti'* can, properly speaking, be neither old nor new, having pre-existed, unaltered, through all eternity. But theological casuistry will thread its way out or worse difficulties. *Smriti, Brahmans* which might be comprehensively paraphrased by "venerable traditions" *which* embraces a vast range of subjects and of time, as we have seen. But there is one set of literature productions of this extensive class which specially belongs to the Vedas, and supplements the Brahmanas and Upanishads. They are manuals on certain principal subject-matters connected with and partly contained in them and which go to the making of the perfect Vedic lore required of every Brahman. These subject-matters are six in number, and, by their nature, show the kind and minuteness of the study to which the Veda *'Word'* or *'Shabd'* especially the Rig-Veda of course which has been subjected from very early times. They come under the following heads:

1. Phonetics (pronunciation and accentuation),-SIKSHA.

2. Meter-CHHANDAS.

3. Grammar-VYAKARANA.

4. Explanation of words (etymology, homonyms and the like)-NIRUKTA

5. Astronomy-JYOTISHA

6. Ceremonial-KALPA.

An exhaustive knowledge of these six things is considered so essential to a full understanding of a Veda and the proper idea of the *infinitely* complicated forms of worship evolved out of the Rig, that they are said to belong to it organically as members to a body, and are very realistically called *VEDANGAS,* "limbs of the Veda", as necessary to its articulate perfection.[3] The several tribes, at first more or less closely related, live, as a rule, on terms of peaceful neighbourliness and hospitality. If quarrels do occur, and lead to armed strife, they mostly arise out of some dispute about flocks and herds, and, at a later time, out of the competition between kindred tribes striving for supremacy or the appropriation of more land. At the more primitive era the principal occasion of warfare was one calculated to tighten the bond of race rather than loosen it, being self-defence, the constant necessity of guarding against the raids of innumerable, lawless hordes of nomads, mostly of non-Aryan stock, who, mounted on their fleet and indefatigable steppe-ponies, kept continually hovering and circling round the pasture land and settlements, whose prosperity excited their greed. Physically, the Aryas, as we can picture them form certain indications, are of high stature, and powerful build, white-skinned, fair-haired, and probably blue-eyed. Ages of seclusion in their first home have moulded these originally local characteristics into a permanent, indelible type, which no amount of uniting with other races will ever be able wholly to obliterate. To the development of this noble *physique* their mode of life is mostly outdoor labour in moderation *world* and their favourable surroundings, must have contributed not a little: a temperate climate inclining to the cold, a land of alternate woods and plains, milk-food in abundance, as well as meat and wheat, pastoral and agricultural pursuits *in* such conditions of existence, if continued through many centuries, undisturbed by intercourse with men of different blood and customs, must result in an exceptionally fine race. Nor are these natural advantages unassisted by art and crafts. The Aryas are prompt and skillful in wielding weapons, which, it is true, are mostly still of hewn and polished stones, shaped and sharpened at an incalculable cost of time and labour, but by no means inefficient for all their clumsiness. Besides, they have lately learned the use of the metals also: gold and silver certainly, and a third metal not fully identified yet *'Word'* perhaps iron. They can fashion and handle a rude sort of plough, which, uncouth as it is, has not only survived its original inventors, but is still in use in more of less remote parts of every country of Europe, owing to the conservatism and stubbornness of the peasantry all over the world, wherever they have not been brought into direct contact and brisk intercourse with the greater of lesser centres of trade and traffic. Their governments are made of skins sewed together or of spun and woven wool. They dwell in houses provided with doors, and surrounded by yards, (or gardens), which simply means "enclosed grounds". They also have hurdles for their cattle and domestic animals as a necessary addition, for they possess very nearly every kind that we own: horses and asses, sheep and goats, pigs and geese, with the dog to guard them, the mouse to pilfer their stores, the wolf and the bear to endanger their folds; they grind the grain, they cook and bake, and have a horror of raw meat. They build boats and skiffs and navigation is known to them, though only. Their minds are open to all impressions, their thoughts are busy with the phenomena of nature, but in abstract speculation they have not yet reached a very advanced stage *still* for they can count only up to the hundred. Such we can picture to ourselves the Aryas, dwelling together as one undivided nation, speaking one language, holding one worship, one mode of life, before they yield to the impulse of migration which has seized on all peoples at certain stages of their existence, when they were separated whether from want of room, or family discords, or the restlessness of awakening curiosity and unconscious sense of power, or from all these combined they begin separate, and detachment after detachment leaves the mother trunk never to return and never again to meet, save in ages to come, mostly as enemies, with no remotest memory of a long severed tie, of a common origin. As tradition itself does not begin its doubtful records till ages after this original separation, and the dawn of the history finds most of the nations which we ascribe to the Aryan stock established on the lands of which they have severally taken possession, it follows that we have just been contemplating a picture, no coins, inscriptions, hieroglyphic scrawls, reach back as far as the time we have endeavoured to retrace. Indeed, the first really historical monuments of any kind at our command are the inscriptions, caused to be engraved in various parts of Hindustan, on pillars and rocks, by ASHOKA, a king who reigned as late as 250 B.C. The same applies to architecture, no buildings or ruins of buildings are to be traced further back than 500 B.C.[4] It was invented, and impression plainly discernible, too, in the prominent place given to the *NAGAS* (snakes and, snake-people, half-human, half serpentine in form and possessed of supernatural wisdom) in the later classical poetry. They play an important part, too, in modern Hinduism, which has instituted yearly festival in honour, not of mythical serpents, but of the real, live snakes, which do not appear to strike this apathetic people with a loathing and terror at all proportionate to the havoc they play with human life.[5] (1.V.I. pp. 293-294. 2. Ibid.; 51-53. 3. Ibid.; pp. 123-125. 4. Ibid. pp. 53-56. 5. Ibid; p. 294.).

13. **Note:** This is a common metre, one-fourth of the Rig-Veda being in this metre. It is so called because the *Gayatri,* the most sacred text in the Vedas, is composed in it. It contains three lines of eight syllables. The first hymn is in this metre. The following is the first verse:

Agnimile purohitam!

Yajnasya devam rtvijam!

Hotaram ratnadhhatamam!!

Macdonell renders this verse in lines closely resembling the original,

'I praise Agni, domestic priest,

God, minister of sacrifice,

Herald, most prodigal of wealth'.

(A.C. Clayton; T.R.V.A.V.R; p. 260). **Note:** Term Gayatri is composed of the Sanskrit words i.e. Gaya+tri; *'Gaya'* means *JANA* in Hindi and 'Go' in English and 'tri' means 'thirst'; when we practice the *'Word'* or *'Shabd'* the thirst of the *mana* slowly and gradually will be completed and *mana* will move towards 'His' house.

14. **Note:** Term Rishi is also composed of two Sanskrit words i.e. 'Ri' means 'route' or way and 'shi' means 'right'. The right way to see the 'God' is the *'Word'* or *'Shabd'.* Such kind of rishi never think about the advertisement. 'He' always keeps mum.

15. **Note:** Vishvamitra is also made of two Sanskrit words Vishva+mitra, *Vishva* means *'World'* and *'Mitra'* means *friend. 'God'* or 'Word', is a friend of the world.

16. **Note:** Term India is also composed of two words i.e. In+dia; 'In' means 'Within' and *'dia'* means *'Light'.* Light is within the body to light-up with the *'Word'* or *'Shabd'* but the Brahmanas are celebrating on earth. It is the limitation of *mana.*

17. V.I.; p. 318.

18. **Note:** Term Vedic is also consisted of two words that is Ve+dic means suspense of mind and heart, they never trust one 'God', or *'Word'.* Because mind or *mana* has been victimized of senses. Senses are the biggest problem of mind or mana. But without the practice of *'Word'* or *'Holy goast',* he (*mana*) can not get peace or solace. It is the challenge of the *'Word'* or *'Nam'* to *mana.* Thus, term Veda is from the Sanskrit Root *'vid',* 'to know', a root which also appears in the Latin *videre,* 'to see', and the English 'wit'. *Veda* primarily signifies 'Knowledge; it designates 'sacred lore' as a branch of literature; and is also applied to the book containing the sacred lore[1]. Till a short time ago, perhaps even at the present day, the popular belief among Hindus as to the origin of Vedas was that they were eternally existent in the mind of the Supreme,

and made manifest by him in each *Kalpa*. The *Kalpas* here referred to are the periods into which, according to Hindu reckoning, the time is divided. Such a Kalpa is a 'day of Brahma' and a 'day of Brahma' consists of a thousand *Yugas* or ages, amounting altogether to four hundred and thirty-two million years of mortals. At the beginning of each *Kalpa* all the existing universe is created and the Vedas are supposed then to be revealed by Brahma through the *rishis*. At the close of the *Kalpa* all the exiting universe is destroyed and then there is a new creation and a new revelation in the new *kalpa*[2]. (1. A.C. Clayton; T.R.V.A.V.R.; pp. 25-26. 2. Ibid; pp. 38-39.).

19. **Note:** VASISHTHA means 'adjectivity'; *Brahmans* or *manas* need advertisement and praises, never think about the humanity. God needs no advertisement, 'He' always do good for everybody. Thus, *mana* take the formation of 'I' means 'ego'. After the death, those do not practice the *'Word'* they will come time and again in the cycle of birth and rebirth. It is the limitation of the Brahma or the Brahmans.

20. V.I.; p. 318

21. **Note:** Term Tritsu is also soothed of two Sanskrit word i.e. Trit+su; 'Trit' means 'Thirst' 'su' means 'love' God has the thirst of love'. He has no thirst of money. Therefore, we must love with the God.

22. VI.; p. 319.

23. *Ibid.*

24. *Ibid.*

25. *Ibid.*

26. *Ibid.*

27. **Note:** Term Sudas is also made of two words i.e. 'Su+das'. 'Su' means 'love' and 'das' means 'thirst'. 'Word' has the

'thirst of love'. When the bard's songs took the form of prayers and entreaties for the favour of the god on the tribe in hunting or war, or for rain in time of drought, or for children to increase the strength of the tribe before its enemies, or for the health in time of pestilence and there was what seemed to be an answer to he petition, the fame of the poet grew great and the wonderful words that had secured blessing were treasured as a spell, or *mantra*, and so it came about that victory in battle was often ascribed to the virtue of some hymn. Thus it is said in the Rig-Veda, VII. 33.3, 'So did Indra preserve Sudas in the battle of the ten kings through your prayers, O Vasishthas. (A.C. Clayton, *T.R.V.A.V.R.;* p. 40).

28. **Note:** Term *Purohitas* is put together of three word *'Pur+O+hitas';* 'Pur 'means 'pious' or 'clear' 'O' stands for "*infinite'* means *'God'* and *'hitas'* means hearts. *Brahmanas* or *purohits* must have the *'Pure heart or thought'* to attain the *'nam'* to quench 'His' thirst otherwise they will remain in trouble that is birth and rebirth. Without the 'pure heart or thought' one cannot attain the beauty of God.

29. V.I. p. 319.

30. *Ibid.*

31. *Ibid.*, p. 320.

32. *Ibid.*, p. 321.

33. *Ibid.*

34. *Ibid.*

35. *Ibid.*

36. *Ibid.*, p. 322.

37. A.C. Clayton; *T.R.V.A.V.R.*; p. 52.

38. V.I. p. 322.

39. **Note:** As to other races that were in the land there is little information in the hymns of the Aryans and the science of ethnology has to help us, from it we learn that before Aryans came India was sparsely peopled by some of races that are now often called 'jungle tribes'. Among them the majority would be Dravidians. The Gonds, Bhils and Santals are modern survivors of those races. Some were very humble in the scale of humanity burying their dead in the cells made of stone-slabs called *Kistvaens* by scientists and *'Pandava vidu'* found in the houses of the Pandava brothers when in exile given by the Tamil people of the south to this day. Those in the south were never so subject to the Aryans as the tribes of the north and grew into the powerful and civilized Tamil and Telugu nations, but there is no hint of this in the Rig-Veda. (A.C. Clayton; *T.R.V.A.V.R.;* pp. 4-6). **Note:** Term *'Pandava'* is composed of two words i.e. *'Pan+dava'* means *'Five words'* and 'vidu' means process. It is the process of the *'five words'* or *'five nad'* called *'Word'* or *'God'*. They are alarming round the clock, but without the *Perfect Master* we cannot attain them. These 'words' are up to the *Perfect Master,* who is present at that time. It has the same process as the "*Five Rivers of Penjab*".

40. V.I.; p. 324.

41. *Ibid.*

42. *Ibid.*

43. *Ibid.*

44. *Ibid.*, pp. 325-326.

45. *Ibid.*, pp. 326.

46. *Ibid.*

47. *"He whom both battle lines call upon in the fray, both adversaries on this side and on that, he whom they invoke, standing on chariots-that, O men, is Indra"* (*II., 12, 8*).

"...The warriors who leagued together against us, whether kindred or strange, break their might". (VI., 25,3).

"Thou, O Indra dost strike both foes, the Aryan and the Dasyu". (VI., 60.6).

"Whatever contemners of the gods, be the Dasa, be they Arya, O glorious Indra, do battle against us, give us an easy victory over them, thy foes". (X., 38,3.).

"Thou (Agni) didst take the goods of mount and plain, and didst strike the foes; both Arya and Dasyus", (X., 69,6). Etc, etc, (V.I. p. 327)

48. The most notable is VISHNU, a solar deity and form of Agni, who holds a very modest place in the Rig-Veda, where he appears as a friend and comrade of Indra, stands by his side at the killing of Vritra, and helps him to 'open the stable and let out the cows". One peculiar trait is attached to him, and mentioned whenever he is addressed or spoken of: he is the god of the three strides. Purely naturalistic-interpreters think of the expression as referring to the strides of the Sun-god to the three stations of his course, at morning, noon, and evening. But closer study shows that there is a far deeper significance behind the seemingly simple myth of *Brahmans* of the three strides of Vishnu cover or pervade, earth, heaven, and the highest world of all, invisible to mortals, as clearly intimated by the verse: "We can form the earth know two thy spaces; thou alone, O Vishnu, knowest thine own highest abode" (*VII.*, 99, 1). However that may be, nothing in the Rig-Veda presages the coming greatness of the god, the future second person Vishnu the Preserver-of The Brahmanic Triad, the rival of Shiva in the devotion of millions of worshippers, till all Brahmanic India became divided into two immense and fanatical sects, the Shaivites and the Vishnuites. It appears, however, that the earliest beginnings of these sects may be faintly traced as far back as the Rig-Veda, from a passage in one of the so-called

historical hymns which relate the early struggles and wars of the Penjab Aryas.[1] And it becomes patent that probably a majority of the common names, which were sweepingly set down as names of fiends and other supernatural agents, really are those tribes, peoples, and men, while many an alleged atmospheric battle turns out to have been an honest, sturdy hand-to-hand conflict between *bonafide* human, mortal champions.[2] The *devas* were at war with *asuras* (the evil demons), who repeatedly conquered them, so that they lost heart, and were main to ask the assistance to Vishnu, the god to whom later theology ascribed the mission of general adviser to the gods and preserver to them and the created worlds. Vishnu promised them that their strength should be restored if they would do as he would direct. First they must collect specimens of all the plants and herbs that grow in the world and cast them into the Sea of Milk, then they must churn that sea, and they would thus obtain the *Amrita,* the drink of strength and immortality. But as the labour would be very great, he advised them to suspend hostilities with the Asuras and invite them to join in the work: "I will take care", he said "your foes shall share you toil but not partake in its reward". The Asuras readily took the bait and worked with all their might. When the herbs were thrown in, the mountain Mandara was taken for a churning sticks (*pramantha*), and the King of Serpents, VASUKI-others say SHESH OR SHESHNA-allowed himself to be used as the rope to twirl the stick. So all pulled with a will, the *devas* on one side, the Asuras on the other, while Vishnu himself, taking the form of a tortoise, took the mountain on his back to steady it. Great was the tumult that ensued. The milky waves rose and tossed and foamed, as though lashed by a mighty storm. Then all sorts of rare, wonderful, and useful things and beings began to emerge from the heaving bosom of that mysterious deep. First rose from them the sacred Cow, then in succession the divine many headed horse, the elephant, a troop of Apsaras (water-maidens), the goddess of beauty appeared, seated on a lotus blossom; deadly poison also was churned out of the waters; Vasuki claimed that as his perquisite, to be given to his serpents. According to some versions the four Vedas also came out of that memorable churning. But on our picture they seem to be represented as one of the divine beings who do the churning water as a person with four heads and four arms, with a book in one hand. Last of all came forth the physician of the gods, radiant, triumphant, bearing aloft the cup with the precious beverage. Both *devas* and *asuras* made a rush for it and there ensued a raging battle. But the *devas* had managed the secure the first drought, and being fully invigorated by it, had no difficulty in beating off their late allies and hurling them into the dark abysses. *See Plate IV, The Churning of the Amrita (Vishnu's Third Avatar or Incarnation-"The Kurma" or Tortoise Avatar)*[3] (Fig. 4). *The post-Vedic Brahmanism, however, retains a vivid memory of a bitter struggle for supremacy between Brahman caste and that of the Kshatriyas. It is given in the form of a story both in the arrogant and oppressive that the interference of Vishnu himself was needed to repress them. The god took human form and was born in the family of the Bhrigu, a priestly race of divine descent, as PARASHU-RAMA ("Rama with the axe") who become the exterminator of the warrior caste." Thrice seven times did he clear the earth of the Kshatriya race and filled five lakes with their blood"-after which he gave the earth to the Brahmans!*[4] The story of the Flood exists in Hindu literature in several versions, always as an incident of some more or less bulky work or collection, except one, which from the subject of a short separate narrative or Purana MATSYA (i.e. "Fish") PURANA means old. It is also given in very abridged form in another of the lesser Puranas the AGNI-PURANA; means old blaze to the Brahmana to collect the money; but the two fullest and most elaborate versions are those in the BHAGAVATA PURANA means old rivalry of the *manas* or *Brahmanas* against the 'Word', one of the most important of these writings, consecrated to the glorification of Vishnu, and in great epic itself, the *Mahabharata*, where it occurs among many legends told on various occasions by this or that learned Brahman, for the entertainment or instruction of this or that royal hero. These versions have been known to Sanskrit scholars for half a century and more, but being found imbedded in such a late, and in some cases almost modern body of literature, representing Hinduism even more than classical Brahmanism, those who had detected the foreign ring of the story were naturally led to attribute it to late Semitic importation, directly connecting it with the Biblical account of Genesis. The surprises was therefore great when a version came to light in one of the great Brahmanas, the SHATA PATHA means 'true way' ("Brahmana of A Hundred Paths"), suddenly removing the legend into an age closely bordering on the Vedic, in which we find it presented, in a monument of distinctly Vedic literature, as an ancient legend accounting for the origin of the present human race. The point of view was shifted at once in a way which necessitated entirely new adaptations, and some peculiar details in the later versions, which will be seen mutually to complete one another, only now won their proper recognition and interpretation. Professor Max Muller published the first translation of the then newly discovered *Shatapatha* version. We here give the latest and most authoritative one, edited and indorsed by the same veteran scholar:

"1. In the morning they brought to Manu water for washing, just as now also they are wont to bring water for washing the hands. When he was washing himself, a fish came into this hands.

"2. It spoke to him the words: 'Rear me; I will save thee. Wherefrom wilt thou save me?' 'A flood will carry away all these creatures; from that I will save thee;-'How am I to rear thee'?

"3. It said: 'As long as we are small, there is a great destruction for us: fish devours fish. Thou wilt first kept me in a jar. When I outgrow that, thou wilt dig a pit and keep me in it. When I outgrow that, thou wilt take me down to the sea, for then I shall be beyond destruction.

"4. It soon become a large fish. Thereupon it said: In such and such a year that flood will come. Thou shalt then attend to me and prepare a ship, and when the flood has risen thou shalt enter into the ship and I will save thee from it.

"5. After he had reared it in this way, he took it down to the sea. And in the same year which the fish had indicated to him, he attended to his advice by preparing a ship; and when the flood had risen, he entered into the ship. The fish then swam up to him, and to its horn he tied the rope of the fish, and by that means he passed swiftly up to yonder northern mountain (Himalaya).

"6. It then said; 'I have saved thee. Fasten the ship to a tree, but let not the water cut thee off whilst thou art on the mountain. As the water subsides, thou mayest gradually descend". Accordingly he gradually descended, and hence that slope of northern mountain is called 'Manu's descent'. The flood then swept away all these creatures and Manu alone remained here.

"7. Being desirous of offspring, he engaged worshipping and in austerities..."

Manu offered much milk-curds and clarified butter *(ghee)*, and in the course of a year, lo! his accumulated prayers and sacrifices took a visible body and stood before him in the shape of a beautiful woman, the divine IDA. He lived with her as his wife, and they became the progenitors of a new race-"this race of Manu", and the Aryan Hindus call themselves. This oldest and simplest version presents only the most general outlines of the familiar story, and if it stood alone it would not warrant any very definite conclusion. We are not even to the fish was, and can only conjecture that it was a divine being or a heavenly messenger. The version of the *Mahabharata* comes next in point of time, it is far more complete, and contains some suggestive particulars. To begin with, we are not left in doubt as to the person of the hero, who is introduced with his usual patronymic, which shows him to be the brother of Yama, as known to us from other sources.

"There was a great Rishi, Manu, son of Vivasvat... (who, through a great many years, gave himself up to the practice of the most fervid religious austerities...)".

"Once a fish came to him on the banks of the Chirini, and spoke: 'Lord, I am a small fish; I dread the stronger ones, and from them you must save me. For the strong fish devour the weaker; this has been immemorially ordained as our means of subsistence. Deliver me from this flood of apprehension, and I will requite the deed.'

"Hearing this, Manu, filled with compassion, took the fish in his hand, and threw him into a jar bright moonbeam. In it the fish, being excellently well tended, grew; for Manu treated him like a son. After a long time, he became very large and could not be contained in the jar. Then, seeing Manu, he said again: 'In order that may thrive, remove me elsewhere'.

"Manu then took him out of the jar, brought him to a large pond and threw him in. There he continued to grow for very many years. Although the pond was two yojanas long and one broad, the lotus-eyed fish found in it no room to move; and again said to Manu: Take me to Ganga, the dear queen of the ocean-monarch; in her I shall dwell'.

"Manu accordingly took the fish and threw him into the river Ganga. There he waxed for sometime, when he again said to Manu; 'From my great bulk I cannot move in the Ganga, be gracious and remove me quickly to the ocean'.

Manu took him out of the Ganga and cast him into the sea.

"When he had been thrown into the ocean, he said to Manu: Great lord, thou hast in every way preserved me: now hear from me what thou must do when the time arrives. Soon shall all these terrestrial objects, both moving and fixed, be dissolved. The time for the purification of the worlds has now arrived. I therefore inform thee what is for thy greatest goods".

"The period dreadful for the universe, moving and fixed, has come. Make for thyself a strong ship, with a cable attached; embark in it with seven Rishis and stow in it, carefully preserved and asorted, all the seeds which have been described of old by Brahmans. When embarked in the ship, look out for me: I shall come recognizable by my horn. So shalt thou do. I greet thee and depart. These great waters cannot be crossed over without me. Distrust not my word'.-Manu replied: 'I shall do as thou hast said'.

"After taking mutual leave, they departed each on his own way. Manu then, as enjoined, taking with him the seeds, floated on the billowy ocean in the beautiful ship. He then thought on the fish, which, knowing his desire, arrived with all speed, distinguished by a horn. When Manu saw the horned leviathan, lofty as a mountain, he fastened the ship's cable to the horn. Being thus attached, the fish dragged the ship with great rapidity, transporting it across the briny ocean, which seemed to dance with its waves and thunder with its waters. Tossed by the tempests, the ship whirled like a reeling and intoxicated woman. Neither the earth nor the quarters of the world appeared; there was nothing but air, water and sky."

"In the world thus confounded, the seven Rishis, Manu and the fish were beheld. So, for very many years, the fish, unwearied, drew the ship over the waters, and brought it at length to the highest peak of Himavat. He

then, smiling gently, said to the Rishis: 'Bind the ship without delay to this peak'. They did so accordingly. And that highest peak of Himavat is still known by the name of NAUBANDHANA ("the Binding of the Ship')

"The friendly fish then said to the Rishis: 'I am the PRAJAPATI BRAHMA, than whom nothing higher can be reached. In the form of a fish I have delivered you from this great danger. Manu shall create all living beings-gods, asuras, men, with all worlds and all things, moving and fixed. By my favour and through severe austere fervor, he shall attain perfect insight into his creative work and shall no become bewildered'.

"Having thus spoken, the fish in an instant disappeared. Manu, desirous to call creatures into existence, performed a great act of austere fervor, and then began visibly to create all living things..."

In this version (not to dwell on its amplification and remarkable literary perfection), three important features are added, which all greatly enhance its intrinsic connection with the Chaldean and Biblical original:

1. The Flood is said to be sent because the time has arrived for the purification of the world or for its punishment, as it amounts to the same thing:

"...The God Ea spoke to me his servants: "Men have rebelled against me, and I will do judgement against them...the heavens will rain destruction...the appointed time has come".

2. Manu is not saved alone, but is allowed to take a few human beings (not his friends or family, but the seven holy sages of Hindu legend and "the seeds".

"...I brought together and stowed into the ship...the seed of life of every kind, my family, my men servants and my woman servants...and also my nearest friends..."

3. The mysterious fish reveals himself to Manu and his companions as Brahma the One Supreme Deity, and speaks to them and bids Manu re-people the world; (Hasisadra is not given any mission or task, but simply translated with his wife into immortal life).[5]

It will be a surprise to many that the Aryan population of the Indian continent should be so out of all proportion small when compared to the descendants and representatives of those races which the Aryan immigrants found in possession. The same difference must have existed on a still greater scale in those earliest times *1320 B.C.* and would alone suffice to stamp as irrational the theory of Aryan supremacy having been established by sheer conquest and force. Of course there was fighting, and raiding, and driving of native tribes into mountain fastnesses, while others were reduced to a state of bondage. But this would account for only a very small portion of the Arya's success; for the laws of overwhelming numerical odds can be defied only within certain limits even by the bravest. But it has ever been one of our race's chief and truest claims to glory, that it has asserted, extended, and maintained its superiority far more by moral means than by physical force. Three agencies were, beyond doubt, mainly active and successful in propagating Aryan intellectual influence and, as a consequence, Aryan material rule: commercial intercourse, foreign diplomacy helped by an innate spirit of adventure, and missionary work. Intermarriages, of course, did the rest. It has always been a characteristic custom among Aryan nations for their warriors to work off their exuberant energies by going forth in search of adventures abroad, frequently in the form of robbing raids or piratical expeditions, but quite as often by taking military service with neighbouring, or even remoter, states or sovereigns, singly or in bands. Opportunities of the kind must have been plentiful with the Aryan youth of Seven Rivers, surrounded as they were with numerous tribes, with whom war must have been a habitual occupation. This naturally paved the way for political alliances, and there were those at whom who were not slow to decide that such was the surest, and in the end quickest way to extend and establish Aryan influence. These were the spiritual leaders of the people, the priestly class which was in time to develop and crystallize into the Brahman caste. In the Rig-Veda we find these most influential persons belonging to families of hereditary poets and bards *Vasishtha* Rishis *Vishvamitra* whose names are handed down as the composers of the sacred humans. Seven of the books in the collection are attributed each to one of these Rishis, who are shown by many allusions and direct assertions in the text to have been attached to the royal families of different tribes where they occupied the position not only of *purohitas* or family priests and national bards, but evidently also that of royal advisers and ministers *for* a custom which meets us as a fully developed and sacred institution all through to the Brahmanic period. But it turns out, on closer inspection, that these royal houses and the tribes they rule, are by no means always Aryan, and it is startling, at first, with our still lingering prejudices, to find an Aryan priest glorying in the position of bard and *purohita* to a Dasyu *mana* i.e. native *"Word"* king and people. Yet we have to get familiar with the fact, which opens out a whole vista of missionary work, conversions, priestly ambition *in abroad* and round national policy. Every one who has lived in India knows 'Word' and the English learned it to their cost at the time of the great mutiny *manas* what almost unlimited influence they wandering home-missionaries have over the population. When such a *guru* (spiritual instructor) makes his sound, the people of the villages which he honours with a visit pour out to meet him and carry him to their homes under demonstrations of respect almost amounting to worship. See Plate V (Fig. 5). Within historical, even modern times, such men have been known to rise to the highest positions at the courts of native potentates, as prime ministers or as unofficial, but all the more powerful, private advisers of the master. Such must have been the Aryan missionaries of the Vedic times, who carried the worship of Agni and Soma into the lands of the Serpent together with Aryan speech and customs. The process of conversion must have been a simple matter enough. A ceremony of initiation significantly named *"a second birth", 'Word'* or *'Nam'* a simple confession of faith practice and the impure brood of the Serpent (*mana*) was transformed into the "twice born" child of bright Devas and admitted into the Aryan spiritual community, the Aryan political confederacy. Now there is in the Rig-Veda a short verse which, under the name of GAYATRI, is to this day considered the most sacred of all texts, endowed with miraculous powers, and has, through over a score and a half of centuries, been separated thrice a day at least, with faith, by numberless millions of human beings. It reads as follows in the translation:

> *"Of savitar the heavenly, that longed for glory may we win, and may himself inspire our prayers". (III, 62.10)*[6]
>
> *Genesis VII.-IX.*
>
> *...And God looked upon the earth, and behold, it was corrupt... And God said unto Noah... I do bring a flood of water upon the earth,... and everything that is in he earth shall die....*
>
> *...Thou shalt come into the ark, thou, and thy sons, and thy wife, and thy son's wives with thee.. And of every living thing of all flash... shalt thou bring in the ark... to keep them alive.*
>
> *And God blessed Noah and his sons, and said unto them, be fruitful, and multiply, and replenish the earth.*
>
> Only with the bombastic exaggeration which has grown on the race since the time of the comparatively sober Veda, he does not limit his command to earth and the human race, but orders him to *create,* besides men, gods, and asuras, and all the worlds. This exuberant imaginative element is still more developed in the version given in the

Matsya (or Fish) Purana, one important feature of which is that the divine preserver is revealed not as Brahma, but Vishnu, a change which could have taken place only after the schism which divided Brahmanism into several sects. One of these had adopted the rather insignificant solar god of the Rig-Veda and invested him with supremacy, as the every watchful preserver and savior of all creation. The Matsya Purana introduces Manu as "a heroic king", the patient son of the Sun, who had attained so high a degree of holiness that he abdicated in favour of his son (name not given), in order to devote himself wholly to ascetic practices, which he kept up with intense fervour during a million year (!) *"in a certain reason of Malaya"* (Malabar). Once, as Manu was offering an oblation to the Pitris in his hermitage, a small fish fell on his hands along with some water. Then follows the incident we are already familiar with: the fish is successively transferred into a jar, into a large pitcher, into a well, into a lake, into the Ganges, and lastly is thrown into the ocean.

"When he filled the entire ocean, Manu said, in terror: 'Thou art some god, or thou art VASUDEVA (It was Vishnu's name). How can any one else be like this? Reverence be to thee, lord of world.' Thus addressed, the divine JANARDANA (Vishnu has "thousand name") in the form of a fish, replied: "Thou hast well spoken and hast rightly known me. In a short time the earth, with its mountains, groves, and forests, shall be submerged in the waters. This ship has been constructed by the company of all the gods for the preservation of the vast host or living creatures. Embarking in it all living creatures, both those engendered from moisture and from moisture and from eggs, as well as the viviparous, and plants, preserve them form calamity. When, driven by the blasts at the end of the you, the ship is swept along, thou shalt bind it to this horn of mine. Then, at the close of the dissolution, thou shalt be the PRAJAPATI ('lord of creatures', in this case 'creator') of this world, fixed and moving."

By "all living things" are certainly meant specimens of each kind, as no ship could have been imagined large enough to contain all individual living things existing, just as "plants" undoubtedly also signifies specimens, or rather the seeds of plants. As for human beings, only one holy Rishi is named by Vishnu as Manu's companion. On being questioned more closely, the god explains that great deluge will be preceded by a universal conflagration which, following on a hundred years of drought and famine, shall consume the world so the earth shall become as ashes and the either itself shall be scorched with heat. Even the gods and the planets shall be destroyed. Of the former only Brahma is to be preserved, of the latter the sun and moon. The Vedas also are to be saved in the ship. An important point on which the story of the Matsys Purana differs from the Chaldean original is that the great cataclysm is not sent in punishment, but occurs as the end of the one *Yuga* or age of the world, ushering in the beginning of another, every such change of period, in the Brahmanic belief, being marked by destruction and resurrection of the universe. The narrative ends rather abruptly:

"When the time announced by Vasudeva had arrived, the deluge took place in that very manner. Then the god appeased in the shape of a horned fish; the serpent ANANTA, means "the Endless"; the symbol of eternity, came to Manu in the shape of rope....He then as he stood upon the ship...."

This same absence of moral point distinguishes the elaborate and dramatic relation in the Bhagavata Purana. Bhagavata-"the Blessed One", one of the most sacred names of Vishnu. This Purana is specially devoted to the glorification of the god and his various incarnations or Avatars.

There also occurs at the end of one of the great ages "an occasional dissolution of the universe", during which the world is submerged in the ocean. But another and, if possibly, greater disaster be falls gods and men: the Vedas are stolen and carried away by "the strong HAYAGRIVA", a demon of the race of the giant DAITYAS, who are forever warring against the god and marring their good works, and it is on discovering this deed that Vishnu takes the form of fish. The human hero of the deluge-incident is not Manu, but "a certain great royal Rishi", called SATYAVRATA, the righteous *King of Dravida,* a devoted worshipper of Vishnu, given to the usual austere practices, and who, in the then following new era, is born again as Manu, son of Visvasvat.

"Once, as in the river Kritamala (a river of the country of Dravida, or Malabar), he was offering the oblation of water to the Pitrs, a fish came with the water in the hollow of his hands".

Here follow the request for protection; the transfer of the growing fish from one receptacle to another, and the recognition of him by Manu as the disguised god Vishnu. To the enquiry why he had assumed this disguise, the god replies:

"On the seventh day after this the three worlds sink beneath the ocean of the dissolution. Compare Genesis vii,4: "For yet seven days, and I will cause it to rain upon the earth... and every living substance that I have made will I destroy...10. And it came to pass after seven days that the waters of the flood were upon the earth..." When the universe is dissolved in that ocean, a large ship, sent by me, shall come to thee. Taking with thee the plants and various seeds, surrounded by the seven Rishis, and attended by all existences, thou shalt embark on the great ship and shalt, without alarm, move over the dark ocean. When the ship shall be vehemently shaken by the tempestuous wind, fasten it by the great serpent to my horn, for I shall be near".

Everything happens as predicted, and when "the dissolution" is over, Vishnu slays Hayagrva and recovers the Veda, while 'King Satyavrata, master of all knowledge, sacred and profane, became, by favour of Vishnu, the son of Vivasvat, the Manu of this era". This is the so-called MATSYA-AVATAR, or *Fish-Incarnation of Vishnu See Plate VI (Fig. 6),* one of ten disguises assumed on different critical occasions by the preserver, to save the world from some great danger, and one of which is yet to come at the end of the present yuga, or era. The Agni-Purana's story though some what more concisely told, is so exactly the same, with no detail added or altered, as not to require quotation. The great French Sanskritist, Eugene Burnouf, who edited and translated the Bhagavata Purana, was familiar with all these versions, excepting only the oldest, that of the *Shatapatha-Brahmana*, which was not known in his time as yet, and he is very positive about the kernel of the story having been imported from Babylon. His only mistake lies in assigning this importation to late historical times, while there is so much, both in the subject-matter and in sundry particulars, that points to an infinitely earlier intercourse, in pre-Aryan times, between the kindred people of Dravidian India and archaic or Chaldean Babylon. The identity between Manu's divine preserver and Ea, the preserver of Hasisadra, is more than accidentally indicated by the fish-disguise of the former, which is also the symbolic form of the latter, as abundantly shown by the monuments, and even appended to the god's name in one of his most momentous incarnations, that of EAHAN (Oannes), the Fish-god, the civilizer of Chaldea.[7] *See Plate VII, (Fig. 7).* As scholarly qualifications and competitive examinations were not dreamt of then as requirements for Indian appointments, it was necessary *for* the good work now inaugurated was not to remain merely the temporary achievement of an exceptions group of men, to be obliterated by the ignorance of their successors *which* has to place that knowledge within every functionary's reach, by transferring it into the English language. This gigantic task resulted in Jone's famous DIGEST OF HINDU LAWS, for which however, he was not permitted to complete, his work and in the translation of the INSTITUTES OF MANU, the code most widely acknowledged in India. This work, the last of a life heaped to overflowing with noble labour, but shortened by the long, never relating strain under a homicidal climate, was published just before his death, in 1790. It had for years been his pet project, and, the better to fit himself for he devoted his few hours of comparative leisure to literary and linguistic studies in the seeming boundless field of Sanskrit scholarship. Once, when so employed, under the guidance of a competent and intelligent Brahman master, Sir William be thought him of a well-known collection of Catholic missionaries' letters about certain "books called Natac" and supposed "certain a large portion of ancient history, without my mixture of fable'. As nothing is so hard to get out all the huge mass of Sanskrit writing as a crumb of real history, he made inquiries, having a strong inducement, as he says himself, in his desire to learn any thing the might in any way be connected with the administration of justice. But he could not make much of the information that was given him, except that those books were not histories but abounded with fables, and consisted of conversations, in prose and verse, on an infinite, variety of subject, and in various dialects of India, "from which he naturally concluded that they were some sort dialogues on moral and literary topics" until a more than usually observant and intelligent Brahman, he goes on to relate, "removed all doubts and gave him no less delight than surprise by telling him that the English had compositions of the same sort, which were publicly represented at Calcutta and bore the name, as he had been informed, of *plays...*" Naturally, Sir William asked which was the most popular of these *Natakas* or asked which was the most popular of these *Natakas* or dramas, and was answered "THE RING OF SHAKUNTALA". Whereupon, he proceeds to tell:

"I soon procured a correct copy, and, assisted by my teachers, began with translating it verbally into Latin, which bears so great a resemblance to Sanskrit that it is more convenient than any modern language for a scrupulous interlinearly version. I then turned it word for word into English, and afterwards, without adding or suppressing any material sentence, disengaged it from the stiffness of a foreign idiom, and prepared the faithful translations of the Indian drama, which I now present to the public".[8]

Thus, nor are such details to be overlooked as that the Manu of the Indian books, whose righteousness and piety make him so exact a counterpart of the patriarchs Hasisadra and Noah, is said to be a *King of Dravida* and is shown performing his devotions on the banks of the river of the land of Malabar, for they conclusively point to the way by which the most notable legend of the old poem of Erech travelled into India long before the future Aryan lords of the country were heard of. That it should have been part of the large mass of native lower incorporated centuries later in the religious literature of the then ruling race, was but natural and it certainly deserves the honour. It is scarcely necessary to point out the identity of the final incident for the stopping of the ship on a high mountain top ("Mountain of the land of Nizir", Mount Ararat, Himavat), followed by the dialogue between the preserved patriarch and his divine preserver, the sacrifices he offers, and the mission given him of re-peopling the earth. But it may be not uninteresting to recall a bit of modern folklore, familiar to us from infancy, yet which it might not occur to one person in a hundred to remember in connection with the venerable old legend, of which, however, it probably is an infinitesimal crumb or chip: the North-German tale of the Fisherman and the Little

Fish, so charmingly told in dialect Brahmana or *mana* as heard from the people *'Word'* by the great Grimm. The beginning, at least, is identical with that of the Manu legend. The fisherman catches a small fish, who begs for life and freedom, promising to requite the merciful deed, whereupon the compassionate fisherman throws him back into his native sea. The sequel, of course, is entirely different: it is a story of human greed and ambition, growing with the indulgence, and finally punished; but the divine character of the Fish is maintained throughout and most vividly, even majestically, brought forth. How many of our favourite and most familiar stories, the humble comforters of cottage and nursery, will be found have wandered down to us by such devious and long-obliterated roads![9] *(1. V.I.; pp. 240-241. 2. Ibid.* p. 303, 3. *Ibid* pp. 188-190. 4. Ibid p. 278. 5. Ibid. pp. 335-340. 6. Ibid.; pp. 314-316, 318, 7. Ibid.; pp. 340-44, 346. 8. Ibid.; pp. 84-85. 9. Ibid; pp. 346, 348).

49. Vishnuism is probably originally connected with the transition from the oldest calender of thirteen lunar months to the reformed solar year of the twelve months, presided over by the twelve Adityas. See Mr. Hewitt's *Early History Of Northern India.*

50. Those worship the *mana,* they are called the sons of the Serpents. It is a comparative study of the Brahmans.

51. Mr. Hewitt,...II, pp. 232, 233 (J. Roy As. Soc. XXI, new series). In the Russian epics cycle there is an evil champion demigod, the constant enemy of the heroes or *bogatyrs,* who goes by the name of "Tugarin the Serpent". Our folklorists have been greatly puzzled to account for the name and where it came from: might the key be found here? (V.I. pp. 328-329)

52. Mr. Hewitt draws attention to this river's name as suggestive of Purus, original home having been on its banks (V.I. p. 329)

53. V.I. p. 329

54. Plate VIII, The Shatadru or Shutudri (Sutlej) (Fig. 8). Collection made from (V.I.) **Note:** Term 'Sutlej' is made of two words i.e. Sut+lej, 'Sut' means 'True and 'lej' means 'Sagar' means ocean or called Heaven on Earth. Go and see the ***'Word'*** live in Heaven practice according to the instructions of the Guru or Spiritual Instructor. Term *guru* is also composed of two Hindi words that is Gu+ru, 'Gu' means 'darkness', 'ru' means 'light' only the Perfect and Present Master can get rid the attraction of life from the 'fiends of darkness' otherwise *brahmans* have to go in the cycle of birth and rebirth. It is the challenge of the ***'Word'*** to the *brahmans*.

55. V.I. pp. 330-334.

PLATES

Plate IV

Fig. 4-The Churning of The Amirta (Vishnu's Third Avatar or Incarnation the ***'Kurma'*** or Tortoise Avatar). (V.I.)

Plate IV

Fig. 8-The Shatadru or Shutudri (Satlej). (V.I.)

Plate V

Fig. 4-Reception Of a Guru Or Spiritual Instructor (V.I.)

Plate VI

Fig. 6-The 'Matsya' Avatar, or First Incarnational of Vishnu In The Form Of a Fish to recover the Sacred Books. Lost During the Deluge. (V.I.)

Plate VII

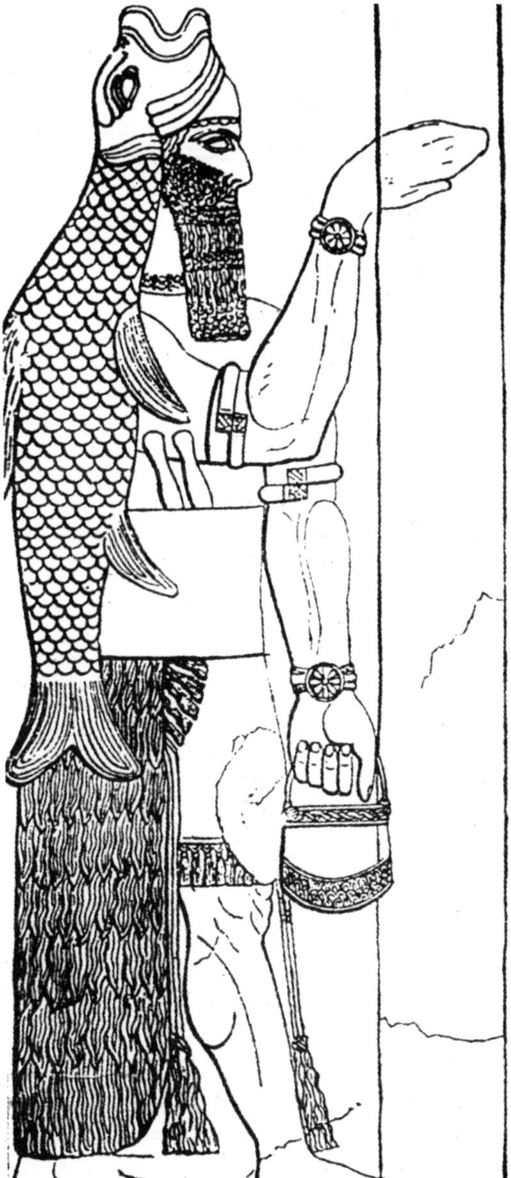

Fig. 7-Oannes........................The God EA. (V.I.)

2

Caste and Reality

The inclusion in the *Veda* of the *Purusa-sukta* which expressly states that the Priest, the Warrior, the Merchant and the Serf were the four orders of men created by divine power is a sign that along with the rise of the Brahman priesthood, there was also arising a distinction of classes in the population which later on became the caste system of Hinduism.[1] It has been noticed that only the three first castes were enjoined to study the *Veda*. No mention of this duty is made among those of the fourth, the servile, caste. But this is not all. The *Shudras* were not only not excepted, they were forbidden, to share the sacred inheritance of those whom to serve was their only mission. Their presence at a sacrifice would have polluted it; the sacred *mantras* were not to be sung or recited within hearing of a *Shudra,* and had a *Brahman* instructed one of the servile caste in the knowledge of the *Veda,* he would have been guilty of wellnigh inexpiable offence. When a boy of one of the three higher castes attained a certain age, considered as "years of discretion." *Any time between the eight and the sixteen year for a Brahman, between the eleventh and twenty second for a Kshatriya, and between the twelfth and twenty-fourth for a Vaishya.* He was "initiated", i.e., admitted under solemn ceremonies into the religious community, after which he was placed under, a *guru* or spiritual guide, invariably a *Brahman,* for instruction in the *Veda.* This initiation was regarded as the youth's second birth, his birth into the spiritual life, wherefore the three higher castes took pride in the appellation of "twice born" *(dvi-ja).* From this distinction the *Shudras,* of course, were excluded. This is declared most explicitly in Manu's Code:

"The Brahman, the Kshatriya, and the Vaishya castes are the twice-born ones, but the fourth, the Shudra, has no second birth. There is no fifth caste."

This brief survey of the original caste system has led us away from what is, properly speaking, our allotted subject, for we have strayed into post-Vedic times. But the digression necessary in order, precisely, to conclude it with the statement that castes, as a firmly established institutions, were not as yet feature of the Vedic period. Had they been, the fact must have transpired, even if indirectly, in the *Rig-Veda,* which faithfully reflects the state of society prevailing at the time that the collection was forming, and this not the case, except in one solitary and note, worthy instance: the ninetieth hymn of the tenth book *(X., 90),* known as the "Purusha-hymn", PURUSHA-SUKTA. The hymn, as a whole, is exceedingly obscure and of entirely mystical import. It describes the act of creation in the guise of a huge sacrifice performed by the gods, in which the central figure and victim is a primeval giant, a being named Purusha (one of the names for man), probably because mankind is represented as being produced by this being or, more correctly, out of various portions of his body. This is the only passage of the hymn with which we are here concerned, Purusha, it is said, "is this whole universe, whatever has been and whatever shall be". Probably in a latent state, since the gods proceed to evolve out of him worlds and animals and men:

"When the goods divided Purusha, into how many parts did they cut him up? What was his mouth? What his arm? What his thighs and feet?"

"The Brahman was his mouth; the Rajanya was made his arms; the Vaishya he was his thighs; the Shudra sprang from his feet".

Now the tenth book as a whole, is a later date than the rest. It was made a sort of receptacle for odd hymns and such as, important in themselves, did not fit well into the scheme of the others, or were attributed to odd authors, while each book (except the tenth and the first) usually bears the name of one priestly poet or family of poets. Intrinsic differences in language, spirit, range of thought, etc., bear witness to the fact. The Purusha-sukta especially comes under this head, and, by bringing the caste system as far back as the late Vedic period, shows how easy must have been the transition from that from the so-called Brahmanic or classical period, there never really having been a violent break between the two. The Brahmanic writings all endorse the Purusha myth with the only difference the Brahma, the Creator and the highest deity of the post-Vedic creed, is substituted for the older name, and the mystic sacrifice is not mentioned. This is why the Brahmans always boast of "the excellence of their origin", their interpretation of the legend being this: that those who came from the Deity's mouth, as the noblest organ, are born to teach and to command; they embody his *Mind,* his word; those that came from his thighs have the mission of carrying and supporting the nobler parts of the social body; while humble service is clearly the lot of those lowly ones who proceed from the divine feet.[2]

In this chapter we hardly used the word which in most minds is most strongly connected with the Hindu social order.[3] Dr. Babasaheb Ambedkar's crusade against caste was a major part of his project to establish the reign of human values of liberty, equality, fraternity and social justice in the Indian psyche. With all his intellectual ventures and studies he found the evil root-cause of all sort of sufferings of the toiling masses, in the caste and the caste system. His life time venture to study the phenomenon of Caste.[4] The term "caste" has been originated from Spanish and Portuguese word *"casta"* meaning, 'lineage or breed'. A.L. Basham has rightly pointed out that the term 'caste' was applied indiscriminately to both *'Varna'* or 'class', and 'jati' or caste proper.[5] Basically, *'Varna'* is a Hindi term; which has been used for its alphabet and in English called 'Word'. The alphabets of various languages of the world are the garlands (*mala*) of the *'Word'* or *'Nam'* and every poet make 'His' poetry. The four alphabets of the English tha is Word', *mana* has been forgotten and wandering in the material world created caste, colour and creed on different patrons. Therefore we must attain the *'Word'* or *'Nam'* from the Perfect Master, who is Present at Bias *"Maharaj Gurinder Singh Ji"* in the form of *Rishi Ved Vyas of the Vedic Age.* The term 'Word' has the beautiful formation 'W' stands for '*Wonderful*'; 'O' stands for '*Infinite*'; 'R' stands for 'round the clock' and 'D' stands for 'destruction', the alphabet 'D' has already been defined in detail in the previous chapter. These *chaturvarna* has the unique theory in the world and 'Wonderful'. It again proves that Sanatan nature of Brahmanical scriptures and their legal authority was based on bias. The term 'Sanatan's primary connotation is itself revealed that 'Sanatan Dharm' was the Dharma of the 'satan' that is *mana* or *Brahmana.*

Although the castes and their names occur but once in the course of entire Rig-Veda, there is another distinction which recurs throughout the collection, no matter to whom the different books are ascribed, and which divides the peoples who dwelt in the Penjab, and, later on, those who occupied the more easterly portion of Hindustan, into two main categories opposed to each other, each comprising numerous sub-divisions, i.e., nations or tribes, many of whose names have been preserved by contemporary bards: this division is that into ARYAS and DASYUS[6] or DASA. Aryas means '*Word*' or '*Shabd*' and Dasyus or Dasa means *mana* 'destroyers' or 'Dasa' or 'injurious',[7] both are kith and kin. Who the former are we know well, and a natural association, leads us to the conclusion that the latter are no other than the native *Arya* or non-Aryan *Brahman* peoples whom the Aryan immigrants found in the land, and whom, after a long period of struggle, they reduced into more or less reluctant submission. There is, no doubt but that we have here the first beginnings of caste, for this sweeping division is singularly like the modern one into "twice born"[8] means '*Die To Live*[9]' in the '*Word*' or '*Name*' and it is a '*Pure-Thought*' or '*Thinking*' called *Shudra* in

Sanskrit. Besides, the name for caste is even now *'varna'*, which means 'colour'[10] but *'Word'* or *'Holy Ghost'* has no colour, 'He' is *'colourless', casteless'* and *'classless'* as mentioned by Dr. Babasaheb Ambedkar in the Indian Constitution. Neither 'He' belongs to Africa nor from America, but now at present in India. It is a *'Dalit Voice'* from the very ancient period, when the history of the man was started and we shall presently see that the difference of colour between the white conquerors and the dark skinned natives is continually alluded to by the Vedic poets. Then, too, the word Dasyu[11], with the changes of meaning it has undergone, tells an eloquent tale. It is an old Aryan *'Word'*, and the Persians continued to use it in its original harmless sense of peoples, nations. In Dareios historical rock inscriptions we find it so used, also in opposition to Aryas, to designate the populations of the provinces. In India it took a hostile shading Brahmans that of "enemies," whence it easily passed into the cloud land of Vedic mythology, with the meaning of *"fiends"*, "evil demons", *Brahman* the power of darkness and drought for the "foes' whom Indra eternally comets and conquers with the help of the Maruts[12], the Angiras[13] and other beings of light. Logical and natural as the transition is, it adds very greatly to the difficulties of Vedic interpretation, because, when Indra or Agni are besought to drive away and annihilate the Dasyus or are said to have destroyed the fastnesses of the Dasyus, it is frequently all but impossible to decide which "enemies" are meant for the earthly or the mythical ones.

How easy and natural the step from "foe" to "fiend" we see from the very word "fiend" which originally meant both. The "arch-fiend" which originally meant both. The "arch-fiend" is the "arch-enemy" of mankind, Era-fiend the Germans call him even yet.

The last change which the word underwent is very significant: it ended by meaning simply "slave, servant", (slightly altered into *dasa*), thus telling of conquest completed, and closely answering the more modern *Shudra*. We may, then, set down as correct the equation: Arya = *'Word'* Dasyu = "twice-born" *modern Shudra*. And if any more proof be wanted of the fact that the servile class was made such by conquest, we have it in a passage of Manu's Code, which forbids the twice-born to associate with a Shudra *"even though he were a king"*. What can a Shudra King be but native sovereign?

It were impossible to exaggerate the loathing and contempt with which the Aryas regarded those whom they were robbing of land and liberty. These feelings primarily aroused by that most intractable and unreasoning of human instincts, race antagonism, find vent in numberless passages of great value, because they enable us to piece together a tolerably correct picture of what those aborigines must have been, and in what manner they chiefly contrasted with their conquerors. The differences in colour and cast of features is the first to strike us, and in that, as already hinted, we trace the beginnings of caste distinction. "Destroying the Dasyus, Indra protected the Aryan colour", gratefully proclaims one poet. "Indra" says another, "protected in battle the Aryan worshipper, he subdued the lawless for Manu, he conquered the *black skin*". "He [Indra] beat the Dasyus as is his wont... he conquered the land with his fair [or white] friends...". Other names given by their Aryan conquerors are "goat-nosed" and "noseless" *(anaso,* evidently an exaggeration of "flat-nosed"), while the Aryan gods are praised for their beautiful noses. The Dasyus are accused of having no sacred fires, of worshiping mad gods, of eating raw meat, and, lastly, it would appear that they were held to be dangerous sorcerers: "Thou [Indra] hast made the Dasa's magic powerless against the Rishi". Needless to add that difference of language completed the barrier which the victors later strove to render impassable.

Although the opposition of Arya to Dasyu or Dasa, of "twice born" to Shudra, is a perfectly established and intelligible fact, it were a mistake to see in "Dasyu" or "Shudra" the names of a particular nation: they applied to all that were not Aryan, somewhat after the manner that, in classic antiquity, all went by the name of "Barbarians" who were no Greeks or Romans. It is suspected that "Dasyu", in a slightly different form, *may* have been originally the name of a people whom the Indo-Eranian Aryas encountered and fought in their wanderings before they entered the Penjab.[14] If so, the name early became a common one for "enemies", then "subjects", and its origin was thoroughly forgotten by both Eranians and Aryas of India. In point of fact, the fair complexioned worshippers of Agni, Indra, and Soma found *two* widely different races in possession. These were undoubtedly broken up into numerous tribes, with different names and under different kings, *non-Aryan* as, for that matter, were the Aryas themselves. The Rig-Veda teems with names which at first produce a bewildering impression of chaotic confusion; but we shall see that the patient labours of a band of ingenious and untiring searchers have already succeeded in bringing some kind of order into this confusion, and evolving out of it something that may be called a twilight of history. This groping in a particularly obscure past, unguided by even the scanties monumental evidence, is materially aided by an observant study of mixed population of India in our own times. "India", writes Mr. Hunter, he who, of living men, has the most thorough and comprehensive knowledge of the immense empire, "forms a great museum of races", in which we can study man from his lowest to his highest stages of culture. "A museum of races" indeed, and no one could say so with better authority than the writer of the above lines, since he complied and published a dictionary of the non-Aryan Languages of India, which comprises 139 language and dialects! Of these but very few, of course, can lay any claim to literary worth; yet the names of several, such a Tamil, Telugu, Kanarese, are familiar to philologists, and hold their well defined place in the lists of important human speeches. They form two groups, representing two distinct and widely different types or families of languages, answering to the two main stocks or races to which respectively belong the various non-Aryan peoples *'Word'* the Dasyus of Vedic antiquity, the *Shudra* of classical Brahmanism, the 'low castes' of Modern 'Hinduism'. See Plate IX (Fig. 9) Brahmans of Bengal (=Aryas), and (Fig. 10) low-caste Bengalese (=Dasyus).[16]

Notes and References

1. A.C. Clayton; *T.R.V.A.V.R.P;* p. 170.
2. *V.I.* pp. 278-281.
3. A.L Basham; *T.W.T.W.I.;* p. 148
4. Dr. Babasaheb Ambedkar; *Annihilation of Caste;* First edition; 15 May, 1936, second; 15th August 2003. Aurangabad (India). p. 3.

5. A.L. Basham *T.W.T.W.I.* p. 148.

6. *V.I.;* pp. 281-282

7. A.C. Clayton; *T.R.V.A.V.R.* p. 6.

8. *V.I.*, pp. 282-283.

9. Maharaj Charan Singh; First edition 1979, 1980, 1983, 1988, 1992, 1995, 1999; Punjab (India). (Study this book in detail for your kind information)

10. *I.V. I.*, p. 283.

11. **Note:** Meaning simply "peoples", "tribes"; a meaning which the word, under the Eranian form DAHYU', retains all through the Avesta and the Akhaemenian inscriptions, while in India it soon underwent peculiar changes, as will be seen. (V.I. p. 113)

12. We already know that the main, most vital fact of India's physical life, that on which it hinges for good or for evil, is the timely arrival and beneficent violence of the south-western monsoon, or, as the unscientific would say, the spring thunderstorms. This is what may be poetically termed the great atmospheric drama, with its incidents of war and conquest its armies and its heroes. Here the imagination of the old Aryas of the Seven Rivers, with there characteristic naturalistic tendencies, revelled unstained. Here, in the Middle-Region Brahmans antariksha *'Word'* was Coludland, which men watched day by day as the familiar but never pallig scenes were enacted over and over again, *now* where INDRA disputed with the Thunderer *'Word'* was *'King'* and the MARUTS-the Storm-winds, Indra's *companion in the Atmospheric Battle* were his friends and helpers; were the clouds were sometimes actors and sometimes scenery, where the precious Cows were fought for, for whose milk the long suffering earth hungers and thrists.[1] Now nothing but a clouds can shed darkness during the day. Agni is asked to

"send the rain-bringing *parjanya* hither"; then the plural is used: "the *parjanya* [clouds] bring joy to the earth". But these are isolated survivals. The Rain-and-Storm god (for India knows little of our quiet rains) is almost always separated from the cloud, which is sometimes his chariot, sometimes the barrel or skin filled with the water which he pours down on the worlds; then he is the "Son of Heaven", who "speaks a gleam-accompanied, resounding 'Word' which brings refreshment". *Parjanya* has one peculiar feature: he pours the seed on the earth; it enters the plants and there becomes the germ. His name is hardly ever mentioned without some allusion being made of this important duty of his, and he is in consequence directly invoked as the special guardian of plants: "Parjanya, who brings us food through the plants". Does not this forcibly remind us of that curious Old-eranian belief that the seeds of all plants were carried down to earth by the rain?[2] Whenever we address our thoughts to the human race of a few thousand years back, we pucker our lips into a superciliously condescending smile, and admire how many fine things our race could do and say when it was so very young and, naturally, ignorant. We should know better by this time; for has not Chaldea *'Word'* to take but one branch which taught us that as far as six or seven thousand years ago great civilizations had not only dawned or begun to bloom, but some had reached and even passed their maturity and were declining into the inevitable doom of decay into which others were to follow them and some, to a certainty, had preceded them. A very little calculation of probabilities will show us that mankind, at the very earliest point at which our eager grasp can secure the first slight hold of it, was *not* young, and when it had reached, say, the cave-dwelling stage, had probably existed, in the dignity of speaking, fire using Man, more centuries than separate it from ourselves.[3] From all this it will be seen that *Parjanya* very possibly goes back to the oldest Aryan period, and might fairly claim a place, in Aryan

India, among the "Older gods", the subject-matter of our preceding chapter. But, with every presumption in favour of the suggestion, which great scholars endorse, the link is broken, direct proof is wanting, no golden beard is violently agitated by the swift motion, as he guides his mettlesome steeds and hurls his bolts around. Again the Maruts. Not much is left to the imagination when they are presented to us as driving chariots borne along with the fury of boisterous winds by their swift tawny horses or dappled deer, and described as follows:

"Spears rest upon your shoulders; ye have anklets on your feet, golden on your breasts, ornaments on your ears, fiery lightning in your hands, and golden helmets on your heads".

Together with Indra they are bidden by Agni, the priest messenger, to the sacrificers banquet, together they quaff huge quantities of the invigorating Soma, and together rush to do battle against Vritra, whom they helped Indra to overcome, to pierce through and through, to cut pieces, till his remains strew the mountain side, and the waters which he imprisoned leap merrily forth, and roll and tumble and pour down on both worlds. Brush and colour could hardly give a more vivid picture at that time and for that picture Indian warrior kings and their gorgeously arrayed body guards have surely sat, it is anthropomorphism running riot. The question is not: how did the hero of the Middle-Region become the war god of men, the champion and protector of his Aryan and native worshipper? but: how could he have helped becoming both? Anthropomorphism, however, seldoms keeps long within such sober bounds *may* certainly not in India.[4] The Maruts themselves are frequently called Rudras. They appear always in troops; sometimes they are twenty-seven, sometimes sixty-six; then there are said to be thousands of them in these ways of laying "a great many". They are all alike; no distinctions are made between them, either of age or appearance; they always act in a body and are "of one mind". Sometimes they drive along "what golden mantles waving, sometimes "cloaked in rain", and once they are shown "clothed in the woolly cloud" as they "split open the rock with might. Their chariots, drawn by self-yoked dappled mares or spotted deer, fleet as birds, now are "laden with lightning", now with buckets and barrels of water which they pour down as they go singing loudly. Their very sweat is rain, and pleasant to the ear the crack of their whips (the whistle and whizz the wind that ushers in a storm). They are boisterous and noisy. The hymns are simply inexhaustible on this theme, and rise on some occasions naturalistic poetry of great beauty. No enemy there to face them, not in heaven nor on earth; this make the mountains to tremble, they rend and show the trees like wild elephants; the earth totters in quakes before them with fear "as an aged king". Of course they are entreated for all the usual giver things of which Indra is commonly the dispel and they are not spared rebuke any more than Indra when they do not respond promptly enough to their votaries' instances:

"Were ye but mortals, O sons of Prishni, and your worshipper were an important-ye should not be neglected as the insect (?) in the grass, nor should ye go the road to Yama [die]; nor be perpetually subjected to distress and danger[5]". (1. V.I., p. 191. 2. Ibid; pp. 195-196. 3. Ibid; pp. 65-66; 4. Ibid; pp. 196-197. 5. Ibid. pp. 210-211).

13. **Note:** The ANGIRAS, another highly reverenced family of hereditary priests and Rishis, are also mentioned in the Rig-Veda as having first kindled Agni. And "Angiras", in the singular, as the name of an individual, is now that of the human but half-mythical ancestor of the priestly race, and now unmistakably a name of Agni himself. The confusion produced by so many names is not as great as might appear at first sight, because one soon detects an underlying general idea, which is neither more nor less

than the kinship between Agni and his mortal worshippers, indeed points to a belief in the celestial and fiery origin of the human[1]. There is another mysterious being, another mother of twins, whose name, *SARAMA*, shows her to be some-what akin in nature to Saranyu, *daughter of Tvashtar, wife of Vivasvat, mother of Yama and the Ashwins,* also a "fleet one", a "runner". With her offspring, the twin *SARAMEYAS* dogs, the messengers of Yama, we are already acquainted[2]. The bare facts are these: Yama was the first to die and we all follow him to the world which he was the first to enter, and where, therefore, he assumed the part of host, receiving those that joined him as they came, and naturally becoming their king and ruler. He has messengers who roam the world spying out those who are to die, and whom they drive or escort to his realm. These messengers, generally two in number, most frequently take the shape of dogs of weird and fantastic appearance, and are probably meant to personify the morning and evening twilight Agni a most apt poetical images, since it can certainly be said that each morning and evening brings some recruits from the living world to that of the dead. It remarkable that the most explicit and pithy text is contained in the Atharva-Veda:

"Him who first of mortals died, who first went to that world, the gatherer of men-King Yama, son of Vivasvat, honour ye with an oblation".

"Death is Yama's wise messenger". A wonderful thought, wonderfully expressed, which we also find in the Atharva-Veda. Birds of evil omen also, are mentioned in the Rig-Veda as Yama's messengers, and one poet prays that the thing which such a bird announces with its cry may not come to pass. The dogs are called SARAMEYA or children of SARAMA and described as spotted, broaded-snouted, four eye and Yama is entreated to bid them protect the guests they bring him on the road. The world over which Yama rules is not repulsive, dark, or in any way dread-inspiring, being situated, as we have seen, in the highest heaven, in the sphere of the sun, in the midst of radiant worlds and no idea of judgment or punishment attaches to it. In the Rig-Veda Yama is the king of the dead, not as yet their judge and chastiser. That came later, and in the Brahmanical literature of the classical period Yama appears stripped of all gracious features and tricked out in all the cheap horrors of the vulgar devil. How different from the mild, benignant deity, to whose gentle rule the earlier Aryan Hindus lovingly, trustfully committed their departed dear ones! The question naturally arises: what natural phenomenon originally was disguised under the myth of Yama Vaivasvata? The answer as naturally suggests itself: the setting sun, for that is one of the scenes in the grand drama of nature which always most forcibly suggested the belief and hope in a future life. *See, for details and texts, Ch. IX, Early Culture, in connection with the Vedic rites.* And in the poetical language of early myth-makers, bristling with bold metaphor, the setting sun can very well be said to be the child of the morning sun (Vivasvat). But then it is by no means sure, as will be seen, that Vivasvat was always the sun, and quite recently a school of interpreters has arisen who would identify Yama, like Soma, with the Moon. It cannot be denied that the arguments they bring in favour of this solution carry a weight. They point out among other things, tha the "seat of Yama" is avowedly in the "third heaven", in 'its most secret (i.e., remotest) place", and that the *setting* sun cannot be said to occupy that position, that the moon easily could appear to the unscientific eye of the early myth-makers as a smaller, *younger* sun, Surya the child of the sun, who dies (disappears) after running his course; that the two, with the in consistency so characteristic of myths, which delight in presenting the same divine beings under different aspects, to place them in different mutual relations, might just as easily have appealed to the imagination as twins *'man'* and *'Nam'* as in point of fact they *have* been considered by most ancient peoples, and that the very name "Yama" is a word signifying "twin". Yama is often spoken of as having been the first man, the progenitor of the human race. But that honour belongs to another son of Vivasvat-*Manu* (i.e. Man), and was mistakenly transferred to Yama, on the strength of an imperfect argument, namely, that he who was the first to die must have been the first man who lived. But Yama is nowhere styled "the first of men", only "the first of the *mortals*". Now the word "mortal" (*martya*) is very frequently used to denote "man"; but two other words-*manushya* and *jana* occur quite as frequently. *It is impossible not to admire the ingenious and phthy names by which those who spoke the ancient Sanskrit tongue designated the human race: martya, "the mortal"; manushya, "the thinking" (the root man being the same as that of mens, mind); jana, "the begotten" "the born" (same root as in gens, genus, generate, etc.).* Yet neither is used when Yama is spoken of. The persistency with which he is called the first of *martyas*, "mortals", is scarcely accidental. Not man alone is mortal in the conception of ancient myth making peoples: the gods themselves would die did they not continually renew their life and vigor by droughts of the divine Soma, the water of youth and immortality; the sun dies when it sets, or faints at the numbing touch of winter; the moon dies when, after waning away before our eyes, it disappears. True, after death comes resurrection; but that does not belong here. We must be content with establishing the fact that Yama is invariably styled the "first of *mortals* who died", not "the first of mortal *men*". Another Vedic deity who can be traced with certainty to a pre-Eranian (or Proto-Aryan) past in VAYU or VATA, the Wind. Not the violent storm-wind, but the wholesome, cooling breeze, that clears the atmosphere, purifies the air, brings health and life to men and animals prostrated by heat. Vayu holds a modest place in the Rig-Veda. Few hymns are addressed to him alone, but he is frequently joined with the other gods, and always mentioned with respect and gratitude. He is a "Son of Heaven" (Dyaus), and not only is he invited to partake of the Soma libations, but when he comes with other gods, the first drink is his by right. There *is, in one of the Brahmanas, a story invented to account for this privilege. It tells how several gods once ran a race for the first drink of Soma, and Vayu (naturally!) won. This is the way in which the Brahmans dispose of all obscure or puzzling points-by stories made up to explain them. The result is generally obscurity doubly intensified, confusion inextricable of philosophy and poetry.*

The following short hymns (X., 168) shows the high esteem in which this unobtrusive deity was held and how sensitively alive the fancy of those ancient poets was to the picturesque and the mysterious 'Word' also how a thing may strike in the same way spirits separated by ages and continents.

"I celebrate Vata's great chariot: it comes rending the air, with noise of thunder. It touches the sky as it goes and makes it ruddy, whirling up the dust on the earth. The flying gusts rush after it,-as maidens to a festivals....- As he flies along on airy paths, Vata never rests on any day....For what place was he born? and from whence came he, the vital breath of gods, the worlds great offspring? The god, wherever he will, moves at his pleasure; his rushing sound we hear, his form was never seen...". "The wind bloweth where it listeth, and thou hearest the sound thereof, but canst not tell whence it cometh and whither it goeth". St. John, iii 8.

With this god we close the cycle of Vedic gods Word' Dyaus, Varuna, Mitra, Agni, Soma, Yama, Vayu, *mana* whom we can trace with absolute certainty to an Indo-Eranian past and identify with corresponding divine beings in the Avesta. Further researches no doubt will bring to light more affinities, more likenesses, *'Word'* or *'Nam'* as indeed not a few have already been hinted at. But suggestions, conjectures, can find no place in work the object of which is to *place* before the larger public interest the uninitiated layman of science-with the results actually achieved, the conquests that may be considered final. The divine personages into whose exalted circle we shall now step are of. Indian growth, bear the unmistakable impress of the land and conditions of life which the migrating Aryas found on the hither side of the Himalaya and the Indus.[3] *Probably on account of her connection with these dogs, Shrama was subsequently made out to be herself a dog.* There is, however, no allusion to this in the Rig-Veda. She herself appears to have been India's special messenger, employed by him on diplomatic and scouting errands. We have an unusually detailed and complete narrative of one such expendition in the Rig-Veda. The Panis, a *mythical robber tribe* the avaricious traders and robbers *Sarama* had stolen the milk kine on which the race of men chiefly depends for *nourishment*. Indra prepared to go to their rescue in company with brihaspati-the Lord of Prayer *Indra's companion in the storm-myth of Sharama and the Panis,* and the nine *Angiras,* the heavenly singers and sacrificers. But he first sent Sarama to reconnoitre. She went "on the right path" and found the strong stable, a vave in the rock, through a cleft of which she heard the cow's lowing. She went on until she came across the Panis-robers, between whom and herself there ensued the following dialogue, one of the most remarkable pieces in the Rig-Veda (*X.*, 108). The Panis begin:

- *The panis: "With what intention did Sarama reach this place? for the way is far and leads tortuously away. What is thy wish with us? Didst travel safely? [or "how was the night?"]. How didst thou cross the waters of the Rasa?" The Rasa-a mythical river, deep and dangerous: the waters of Darkness or of Death.*

• *Sarama: 'I came sent as the messenger of Indra, desiring, O Panis, your great treasures. This preserved me from the fear of crossing, and thus I crossed the waters of the Rasa".*

• *The Panis: "Who is he? what looks he like, this Indra, whose herald you have hastened from a-far? Let him come here, we will make friends with him, then he may be the herdsman of our cows".*

• *Sarama: "Ye cannot injure him, but he can injure, whose herald I have hastened from afar. Deep rivers cannot overwhelm him; you, Panis, soon shall be cut down by Indra".*

• *The Panis: "Those cows, O Sarama, which thou cam'st to seek, are flying round the ends of the sky. O darling, who would give up to thee without a fight? for, in truth, our weapons too are sharp"*

• *Sarama: "Not hurtful are your words, O Panis, and though your wretched bodies were arrow-proof, though the way to you be hard to go little will Brihaspati care".*

• *The Panis: "That store, O Sarama, is fast within the rock-it is full with horses, cows, and treasures; Panis watch it who are good watcher: thu art come in vain...".*

• *Sarama: "The Rishis will come here, fired with Soma, Ayasia, and the Angiras, the Nine. They will divide this stable of cows. Then the Panis will spit out this speech. [wish it unspoken]".*

• *The Panis: Of a surety, Sarama, thou art come hither driven by the violence of the gods: let us make our sister; go not away again. We will give thee part of the cows, O darling".*

• *Sarama: "I know nothing of brotherhood or sisterhood; Indra knows it and the awful Angiras. They seemed to me anxious for their cows when I came; therefore get away from here, O Panis, get far away".*

Sharama's scouting having proved more successful than her diplomatical effort, she returned to those who sent her, to act as guide. Swift and sure of foot, she walked before them, taking them along the broad and ancient heavenly path which leads to the one goal. As they approached the rock, which she was first to reach, the loud singing of the *Angiras* mingled with the lowing of the cows in the cave. Indra and Brihaspati now came up, the rock opened with a great crash under the blows of Indra's mace, and Brihaspati led forth the cows, driving them along as the wind drives the storm cloud. The Panis were dismayed; VALA, the ave-demon, mourned for his beautiful cows as the true mourns for its foliage when it is stripped bare by frost. *The narratives is given in words turn-on from the Rig-Veda, only the passages are so short and scattered, it would be cumber-some to give chapter and verse for them all. This particular myth, with the active part of Brihaspati plays in it, was a great favourite, for active part of Brihaspati plays in it, was a great favourite, for it is alluded to innumerable times, though Sarama is mentioned only in half dozen texts.*

This beautifully and dramatically developed story-myth speaks for itself, and it is only the identification of opinions. She, too, has been said to be the Dawn, and the storm cloud; but she is so specially characterized as the precursor of a violent thunder-storm that, if a naturalistic interpretation be adopted, *'Nam'* no doubt the original one *man* one is more tempted to concur in that which makes her out to be the wind which precedes a heavy rain. It is only the wind that can be called the scout of the heavens; only the wind that may be said to try to bring away "the cows" from the solid black mountain banked up against the horizon, and to be unable to accomplish it until the storm-god and his troop follow the "broad trail" opened for them and break open the rock. This explanation is greatly confirmed by the fact that Sarama's canine offspring, the Sarameya dogs, undoubtedly are the evening twilight twins (probably in symmetrical opposition to the morning twilight twins, the Ashvins), who have inherited their mother's scouting and cattle-driving qualities,' only the cattle they are after are men, and most certainly represent the twilight *together* with and inseparably from the breeze which, in Southern climes, invariably rises immediately after sunset.

The name Sarameya has been philologically identified beyond a doubt with that of the Hellenic god Hermes, the messengers of the gods the sweet whistler and musician, the stealer of cows and guide of the dead-and Hermes is certainly the wind.

That, like the Ashvins, these twins may, in the course of time, have been separated into morning and evening, is more than likely, indeed one Brahmana, in one of those rare passages of profound poetical beauty ("rare" in every sense of 'Word'), which reward the patience searcher, calls Day and Night, "the outstretched arms of Death". So much for this most lucid nature-myth. But nature-myths have a way of becoming transformed in the course of time; and if they do not actually descend to earth and become the stories of the old-times heroes and sages, they dan undergo changes to suit the developing spirit of the race and age without being taken from their celestial habitat. This appears to have been the case with the myth of Sarama, even before it assumed its fixed and finished form in the cannon of the hymns. For in this form latest research finds good reason to see a combination of nature-myth and spiritual, or rather ritualistic, elements, introduced by those all pervading priestly influences which were soon to culminate in the tyranny of Brahmanism. In this transformed myth Sharama represents no longer a power of nature, but that of the human Prayer, more correctly the scared 'Word' i.e. the *mantra,* for, as early as the Vedic times, prayer was no longer the spontaneous outpouring of the heart, as it must have been at least sometimes and with the some of the first composers of the hymns, the ancient Rishis, but a strictly regulated reciting of texts considered as sacred and powerful in themselves, with a sort of talismanic power, and credited with compelling force to over the elements, i.e., the gods. It will be seen that Sarama, as a personification of this Prayer, can well be imagined as "going on the right path" ("the path of *rita",* represented on earth by the sacrifice rite), "finding the cows", frightening the robbers, then guiding the god to the strong stable and standing by while he breaks it open. This secondary interpretation will be very convincing if we consider who Indra's attendants are on this occasion: not the Maruts, but the *Angiras mana* a troop of priestly demi-gods, supposed to be divinized ancient sacrificers, in reality themselves personifications of the sacred hymns which they go on everlastingly singing on their aerial way. Now the heavenly form of the sacred song is the voice of the thunder. When the loud singing of *the Angiras* mingles with the lowing of the captive cows, of course we know we have to imagine the long swelling and rolling thunder of the southern storm, answered by muffled mutterings from the distant mountains, while the "loud crash" with which the cave-stable is burst open is the short rattling clap of the bolt that strikes. For all heavenly music is produced either by thunder or the wind or the rain. And thunder is the *'Sacred Word' the Sacred Hymn par excellence.* The prototype of all speech, the language known to gods, but not understood of men.[4] This beautiful and natural solution is suggested by the results of latest researches, *see chiefly Hillebrandt Vedische Mythologie, Vol., pp. 99-100. It will be noticed that Helmend ends, not in a sea, but in a large lake, to which the name of Samudra would apply perfectly,* and confirmed from a most unexpected quarter by a curt mention in the

Atharve-Veda (VI., 100,) of *three Sarasvatis 'Word'* a mention which, being long unexplained, has been another of the puzzles which confront scholars at every steps. Probably no explanation was needed at that time, of things which has not passed out of remembrance. Sarasvati in post-Vedic times is chiefly praised invoked as the goddess of eloquence, though see never lost her identity as river-goddess. We ourselves speak of "a rich, a free, an easy flow of words", of "fluency of speech", of a "torrent of eloquence", Brahman so that poetical imagery which underlies this transformation will not appear far-fetched or strained. In the Rig-Veda we do not yet find her thus specialized, but she is associated with sacrifices and the hymns in a way to leave little doubt that, in the later portions of it, she already represented the eloquence of sacred poetry, possibly even the different sacred metres which were extolled and deified to such an extra ordinary extent in the Brahmanas. The same may be said in a still greater measure of another goddess, VACH, *ch* pronounced as in *church* personified Speech, '*Word'* who in the Rig-Veda already (in the late book of course, the tenth) is invested with much of the usual pomp of Brahmanic metaphysics, as a "most adorable", "widely pervading", wealth bringing deity of "many abodes", but not to extravagance; the personification *'Word'* or rather allegory. *mana* does not pass the bounds of fine, even 'noble' poetry, and is moreover distinctly traceable to the natural phenomenon from which it is evolved. For sublimity, few conceptions can equal this of our race's earliest poets-a conception which lingers still in the mythical poetry of later nations in other lands. Primeval speech is the voice of the gods, speaking in thunder and storm; it is *Vach... ch.* the *'Sacred Word',* majestic and compelling, beneficent and wise *'Nad'* in its heavenly abode. But it is not for men. To them Vach descends in the form of Speech, and lo!

"1....Men with their earliest utterances, gave names to things, and all which they had lovingly treasured within them, the most excellent and spotless, was disclosed.

2. Wherever the wise have uttered speech [Vach] with discrimination, sifting it as meal with a sieve, there friend knows friend and auspicious fortune waits on their words.

3. Through sacrifice they followed the track of Vach, and found her entered into the Rishis. Taking her, they divided her into many portions, and now the seven Rishis sing her praise.

4. One man, seeing, sees not Vach: another hearing, hears her not; to another she willingly discloses herself, as a well-attired and loving wife displays her person to her husband.

5. One man is said to be secure in her favour-and he is not to be overwhelmed in poetical contests; another lives in unprofitable brooding; he has only heard Vach, and she is to him without fruit or flower.

6. He who for sakes a well-meaning friend, he has no portion in Vach, and what he hears, he hears in vain: unknown to him is the path of virtue.

7. And even those who enjoy her with equally understanding eye and ear, are unequal in the moving of the spirit: some are lakes which reach up to shoulder and to mouth, and some are shallow waters good to bathe in.

8. When competing priests practice devotion in saying born of the spirit's might, one lags far behind in wisdom, while others prove themselves true priests.

9. One sits and produces songs like blossoms; another sings them in loud strains; one-discourses sapiently of the essence of things; another measures out the sacrifice according to the rite.

10. And friends are proud of their friend, when he comes among them as leader of the poets. He corrects their errors, helps them to prosperity, and stands up, ready for the poetical contest". (X. 71)

The beauty, dignity, and ennobling uses of speech cold scarcely be appraised with finer feeling or after touches; or the difference between him to who seeing, sees not, and hearing, hears not, and him to whom the gift is given between the spirit deep as the lake and the mind shallow as the bathing pool, between him who blossoms into song, and him who unprofitably cudgels his brains and for whom the goddess has neither fruit nor flower. Only, we must beware of putting more modern a sense into passages of this kind than they will bear. We must remember that the poetry we have to do with here, though god-given, is not the free, unfettered gift that it is to us: the goddess must be sought *through sacrifice,* which means that she comes loaded with all the shackles of rite, ceremonial, sacred metres, etc. The poetical contests are for the composition of hymns, the errors which the victorious priest corrects are errors in sacrificial *technique,* the prosperity to which he helps is that obtained, nay compelled, from the gods by correctly regulated prayer *(Brahma).* Still, the poet who "fashioned" this hymn, builded better than he knew, and, if freed from extraneous, priestly matter, it remains an exquisite thing for all time. Not so another hymn (X., 125) consecrated to Vach, where the goddess is the Brahmanic abstraction and nothing more, or that most characteristic passage where she undergoes the inevitable transformation into a cow. The poet is discontented. Maybe he is *purohita* to a prince who is not over lavish the sacrifices-which are expensive-and fees and gifts have been coming in scantily. He puts his plaint in the mouth of the goddess Vach, whom he presents as saying:

"I, Vach, the skilled in speech, who assist all pious practices. I, the divine cow who has come from the gods, I am neglected by evil minded man".

We will conclude over selection with a short poem (it can hardly be called a hymn) in praise of Aranyani, the goddess of forest solitude *(Waldein-samkeit)*, or rather-the personified Forest. Not that she is of much importance as a divine being, indeed she appears to have been invented for the occasion by some poet-hermit whose soul was attuned to her mysterious charm. But it is a pretty thing; and besides, it shows that forest life, which was to become so distinctive a feature of later Brahmanism, is-like almost everything that ever held place in the spiritual life of Aryan India, *'Word'* to be traced to the fountain-head of it, the Rig-Veda. We must imagine the thousand strange sounds and delusions which seem to encompass the solitary listener of an evening in the darkening forest:

"1. Aranyani, Aranyani! thou seemest to have lost thyself there: why dost thou not ask the way to the village? Does terror not seize thee?

"2. When the owl's shrill call is answered by the parrot which hops about as though to cymbals 'rhythm, then does Aranyani rejoice.

"3. Here, there is a sound as of browsing cows; there, houses appear to be seen; then there is a creaking at eventide, as though Aranyani were unloading carts.

"4. Here one man calls to his cow there another fells a tree; then one dwelling in the forest at night fancies that some one else has screamed.

"5. Aranyani is not herself murderous, if no one assails (a tiger etc.); and after eating of sweet fruit, a man rests there at his pleasure.

"6. I sing the praise of Aranyani, the mother of wild beasts, the spicy, the fragrant, who yields abundance of food, though she has no hinds to till her.[5]

Brahmanspati or Brihaspati: Then '*Sabad*' Indra's companion. It is not Vishnu, or Soma, or even Agni in his direct natural form; it is BRIHASPATI or BRAHMANASPATI-Fire in his most august, sacrificial, and sacerdotal form, the "Lord of Prayer," the leader of hymns, the institutor of worship and rites; in a word, the divine *hotar* and *purohita,* the priest of god and men, having himself the name of "Angiras" Brahman the leader of the Nine, and the divine personification of both the holiness and the power of *brahma-Prayer,* as represented by the sacred songs-*saman,* or *sacred texts-mantra. Brahma, from a root meaning "to penetrate, to pervade, it is also contained in the name of Brihaspati'.* When therefore he is called *pathikrit-"path*-prepare". *The exact equivalent of the Latin highest priestly title pontiff literally "bridge maker". Pons, pontis* originally meant not a bridge, but a path: a bridge is a path across a river. *The Tentonic and Slavic languages have retained the old meaning.* Thus we are not puzzled as to what path is meant: it is the same that "the old Rishis have prepared", that on which Sarama led the gods, the broad and ancient heavenly path which leads to the one goal, the path of Sacrifice. In the hymns addressed to this priestly deity, he is credited with all the deeds and works elsewhere ascribed to Indra and all the other great nature-gods, whose supremacy thus seems to be centered in him or rather transferred to him, and numberless short interpolated passages bring him into older hymns where he is manifestly out of place. Indeed we have in him the connecting link between pure Vedism and rising *Brahmanism.* For not only are the Brahmans the men who wield the power of the *Brahma,* but the line of abstract speculation, initiated by this creation-and reflection-of the priestly class (soon to be a caste), gradually suspersedes the old joyous, vigorous nature-worship, and culminates in the evolution of the *brahma* (neuter noun) into an all-pervading but latent spiritual essence and presence, and its final manifestation in the person of the supreme god and creator BRAHMA (masculine), the head of the great Brahmanic Traid. It has been remarked that "all the gods whose names are compounded with *pati* ["lord of"] must be reckoned among the more recent. They were the products of reflection". It should never be forgotten, at the same time, that such secondary mythical persons (abstractions) must of necessity have developed out of primary ones (nature gods), and the Rig-Veda shows us exactly how it was done. "Brahmanaspati" is repeatedly used in the hymns as an adjective as epithet of Agni. It does not follow from this that, after the epithet is detached from the name it qualifies and has becomes a separate person, that person should be considered as always identical with the bearer of that name, for with an individuality it also assumes individual life, and begins its own course of evolution, but the original connection between the two will always be apparent, as that of Brihaspati with sacrificial fire. Thus again Savitar. Soma, Indra, each in turn receive the epithet of PRAJAPATI-*'Nad'* "lord of descendants", or, as the 'Word' is more commonly translated, "lord of creatures". In the late stage of Vedic theology, the dawning era of abstractions, we always have *Prajapati* mentioned, and occasionally invoked as a separate deity. It is only in post-Vedic Brahmanism, however, that he attains the supreme honour of being identified with Brahma himself. Another connecting link; another product of the period of transition. Such also is VISHVAKARMAN "the fabricator of the universe", originally a title given to Indra, Surya, and other great gods, then an independent deity, tending, in true Vedic fashion, to absorb the functions, qualities, and honours of all other gods. Two hymns are consecrated to him (X., 81 and 82), where he is described as:

"The one god who has on every side eyes, on every side a face, arms, feet; who, when producing heaven and earth, shapes them with his arms and wings...Who is our father, our creator, maker,-who ever place doth know and every creature,-by whom alone to gods their names were given, to whom all other creatures go, to ask him"

Among these gods of the second formation we may also class *HIRANYAGARBHA, "the Golden Embryo",* or "the Golden Child", evidently originally a name of the Sun, who goes the same way of abstraction which leads these gods to the supreme rank. A most beautiful hymn (X., 121) is addressed to him, but is properly belongs, as well as greater portion of those of Vishvakarman, among those that illustrate the beginnings of speculative philosophy in the Rig-Veda.[6]

It is peculiar that the direct question is never asked: *"Who made the world"* or worlds-but only how it was made: how "they" made it, or-in the latest stage, when philosophical abstraction has reached the conception of one *creator (a dhatar, a prajapati, a vishvakarman)* how he made it, and *out of what.* This particular question fully thought out and adequately worded, we encounter in two speculative hymns, of Book X, addressed one to "all the gods" *(vishvedevah) and again Vishvakarman,* "the artificer, or fashioner, of the universe".

"What indeed was the wood, what the tree, out of which they fashioned [after the manner of carpenters] the heaven and the earth? these two stand fast and grow not old forever, while many days and mornings pass away" (X., 31,7.).

"What was the standing-place, what the stable support, the position, and how was it, from which Vishvakarman, the all-seeing, produced the earth and disclose the heaven by his might?... What indeed was the wood, what the tree out of which they fashioned the earth and the heaven?

Inquire, ye wise ones, with your minds, what it was on which he took his stand when he made fast the world" (X., 81, 2 and 4).

These verses are found in the Yajur-Veda also, and one of its commentaries the Taittriya Brahmana answers the question thus:

"*Brahma [neuter] was the wood, Brahma was that tree out of which they fashioned the heaven and the earth. Wise ones, with my mind I declare unto you, he took his stand on Brahma when he made fast the world*".

Perhaps as good an answer as the subject will admit, at this transition stage from Vedic naturalism to the spiritualism and pantheism of the Upanishads the stage when the Brahma is already felt as the universally present, latent life and force, which, manifested, becomes both matter in its tangible form and spirit in its active working, but not yet as the One, self-existing Soul of the all and Creator of the world. Like all the phases of the thought recorded in the Rig-Veda the ideas on the making of the world pass before our eyes through several progressive stages, the first and the simplest of which is well represented by this statement in one of the Vasishtha hymns: "Varuna stemmed as under the wide firmaments; he lifted on high the bright and glorious heaven; he stretched out apart the starry sky and the earth" *(VII.,* 86, 1). The same things are said of other gods also. But when it comes to details, three distinct conceptions crystallize out of hundreds of texts bearing on the *subject:* (1) the gods *built* the world, carpenter-fashion, as the Aryas built their houses; (2) the gods-this or that couple, especially Heaven and Earth or the gods generally 'Word' gave *birth* to the world, after the manner of living beings: (3) the world was created through Sacrifice, as by Sacrifice it is kept going. The first of these conceptions may be classed almost entirely under political imagery; the second, in great part, with an evident but rather clumsy flight into symbolism; while the third, purely theological, soars into almost unattainable regions of abstruse mysticism. This is the conception so amply developed in the preceding chapter, and the final consecration of which will be given a few pages further.[7] (1. *V.I.,;* p. 165. 2. Ibid. p. 256. 3. Ibid. pp. 182-187. 4. Ibid: pp. 256-261. 5. Ibid. pp. 269-273. 6. Ibid. pp. 261-264. 7. Ibid. pp. 415-417.).

14. **Note:**. *Nor were these "enemies" always and necessarily of non-Aryan stock. The Dahae (possibly the original "dasyus") seem to have been "a tribe nearly akin to the Eranians", located "in the Kirghiz-Turkman Steppe, which extends from the Caspian sea beyond the Yaxatres (now Syr-Darya)". See Ed. Meyer, Geschichte des Alterthums, Vol.$ 425. P 525, and Hillebrandt, Vedische Mythololigie, Vol. I, pp. 94-116. In this most important chapter it is also suggested to identify the wealthy robber tribe of the Panis with the Parnians, whom the Greek biographer Strabo describes as nomads a sort of Eranian Bedouins having their abodes along the Oxus (modern Amu-Darya), and that of the Paravatas or "Mountaineers", a people whom the Vedic Aryas fought, with the Parouctai, dwelling in the mountains, also of "foreign" Aryan stock (Ibid pp. 97, 98)* (V.I. p. 286.).

15. Plate IX, (Fig 9) Brahmans of Bengal. (=Aryas). (Fig 10) Low Caste Bengalese (=Dasyu). **Note:** Term 'Aryas' is used for 'Word' and 'Dasyu' for *mana* or *Brahmana*. "Word" is *'Wonderful Power'* and *Brahmans* or *manas* are *'Black Power'* or *'Evil Power'* attached, with the material world which is always destructive created, caste, colour and creed as a barrier in the society and has forgotten the *'Ultimate Reality'* that is 'Word', and constructing standards types of Hindu 'temple' *(mandir)*, which has persisted from the 6th century A.D. to present day. [1] Basically, word 'temple' has been originated Latin word 'templum', open or consecrated space that space is the flat part either side of

the head between the forehead and the ear according to old French, is the house of god, and term *'mandir'* which is composed of two words i.e. 'man+dir' *man* means *Brahmans* or *mana's*, 'dir' in Indian languages we shout on dog on his different activities. It is the condition of the *man* or *brahmans* in this universe without *'Nam'* or *'Word'*. The heart of the *mandir* was a small dark shrine-room means 'friends of darkness', called *'garbhargrha'* means 'house of the ego' which is destroyer or injurious. This opened on a hall for worshippers *(mandapa)* means *man, 'dapa's* "cover of the darkness" from the *'antarala'* period means from the very long time and taking shelter over the entrance of a building called *'ardhamandapa'* means which has been made by the *brahmans* or *manas* covered by the *"fiends of darkness"*, was not fundamentally different from that of the ancient 'Greeks'. Term 'Greek' is also composed of two English term i.e. 'G'+ 'reek' 'G' stands for 'good' and 'reek' means having a very unpleasant smell or 'giving out smoke' at present[2] to the society. (1. A.L. Basham; T.W.T.W.I.; p. 356. 2. Ibid.).

PLATE

Plate IX

Fig. 9-Portrait of Brahmans Of Bengal (=Aryas)

Fig. 10-Portrait of Low-Caste Bengalese (=Dasyu) (V.I.)

3

History of Kshatriya

Everybody knows what is meant by caste system in India. The second class was ruling one, the members of which were in Rig-Vedic period was called Kshatriya.[1] *The theoretical duty of Kshatriya, he commanded to "protect the people", to bestow gifts, to offer sacrifices, to study the Veda, and to abstain from attaching himself to sensual pleasures.*[2] The human race sprang from Manu and his family, the survivors of the great flood. Manu had nine sons, the eldest of whom was a hermaphrodite-hence known by a dual name Ila. From this son arose the two main lines of royal descent, the Solar dynasty *(Chandravamsha)* from Ila.[3] To begin with plain fact, SURYA is the Sanskrit common noun designating the Sun, the root contained in it gives it the meaning of "brilliant, shining". And Surya is, in the Rig-Vedic, the material, visible luminary, "created" by the gods (or even some particular god), and obedient to their bidding. But Surya is not only the sun, he is also the Sun-god, powerful, independent, subject only to the ordinances of the great Aditiyas, themselves governed by *Rita,* the supreme Cosmic and Moral Law. This distinction *mana* surely unconscious, and which we find in the presentment of all the Nature gods '*Nam*' or '*Kalma*' between their physical and moral essence, accounts for the difference in the tone of the several hymns, addressed to this deity. These invocations are mostly fine poetry, and the figures used explain themselves. One quality has been universally ascribed to the divinized Sun in every age, by every ancient race: that of being "all-seeing". The association of this quality with the giver of light and the disperser of darkness is too natural to suggest a mutual borrowing, and we need not wonder if we find a striking resemblance between the Old Chaldean and the Old Aryan hymns to the Sun, not only in this particular but in several other poetical conceptions. Surya, a Son of the Sky (Dyaus), we have already learned to know as the Eye of Mitra and Varuna.[4]

Once Surya is called the Eye of Agni also and now, in Oriental phraseology, the Eyes of the King are his spies, so it is but natural that he should observe all the deeds of men, and report them to the great Aditiyas, the guardians and avengers of Law and Right. That the expression was really understood in this manner is proved by the frequent prayer to Surya to "report men sonless before the Aditiyas" Word which looks singularly like a request, in child-slang, "not to tell on them", and so not bring them into disgrace and punishment. Thus one of the Vasishthas sings:

"If thou, O Surya, at thy rising wilt report us truly sinless to Varuna and Mitra, we will sing to please the gods... Surya is rising, O Varuna-Mitra, to pace both worlds, looking down on men, protector of all that travel or stay, beholding right and wrong among men. He

unharnesses his seven HARITS. Surya's seven steeds or mares-as also the Dawn's-are generally called HARITS ("brilliant ruddy"); they are of course his rays, as the first verse of 1., 50, expressly shows, and hastens dutifully to your throne ye twain, surveying all beings, as a shepherdhis flock... Surya emerges from the sea of light, he whose path the Aditiyas laid out....It should be noted, however, that the steeds of other gods Indra's and Agni's for instance are also sometimes called so...." (VII. 60).

"...He unweaves [ravels up] the black mantle, his rays cast off the darkness; rolling it up as a hide and dropping it into the waters."

"Not hanging on to anything, not made fast, how comes it that he falls not from such height? By whose guidance does he travel? Who has seen it?" (IV. 13)

Even more rapturous is the following greeting:

"The gods bright face has now arisen, the Eye of Mitra, Varuna, and Agni, Surya fills heaven, earth, and atmosphere, the breath of life of all that stand and moves... The beautiful golden Harits, the bright ones, hailed by songs of joy, they mount to the highest heaven, and in one day their course encircles heaven and earth... And then he unharnesses the mares, the veil of darkness spread over all things" (1. 115)

We have learned to know the Sun as a horse, and as a bird. These images both remain standing symbols of the god, and there even are two hymns (1, 163 and X., 177), rather obscurely and mystically worded, celebrating him as "the Bird adorned by the Asuras"

(Varuna), and as "the Horse who neighed as soon as he was born, emerging out of the water [or mist]", the Steed with the "falcon's wings and the gezelle's feet". So the Dawn is said to bring "the Eye of the gods" to "lead forth the white and lovely horse". There are few entire hymns addressed to Surya, but of these the following (1., 50), has become famous for its rich imagery and its unusually finished literary form:

"1. The gods who knows all beings rises aloft, drawn by his rays, that he, Surya, may behold all things," that all may behold Surya.

2. Straightway, like thieves, the stars with their brightness slink away the all-seeing god.

3. His rays are visible to all mankind, blazing like flames.

4. All conspicuous on thy rapid course thou createst light, illumining the whole firmament.

5. Thou risest for the race of gods and for that of men, that all may behold thy light.

6. With that same glance wherewith Varuna, the illuminator, surveys the busy race of men.

7. Thou, O Surya, searchest the sky and the wide space, making the days, spying out all creatures.

8. Seven mares bear thee on, O farseeing Surya, in thy chariot, god of the flaming locks.

9. Surya has harnessed the Seven Harits, daughters of the car, self-yoked.

10. Gazing out of the darkness up at the highest light, we have reached surya, a god among the gods."

Relations of Indra and Surya: Surya's relations to Indra are rather peculiar. The grim warrior god appears to treat him sometimes in friendly and sometimes in a hostile way. True, there are many passages-in hymns to Indra, be it noted-which would place the sun-god in his direct dependence, by actually saying that he was *created* by Indra, but this must be taken only as a piece of exaggeration from excessive zeal on the part of the worshipper to ingratiate himself with the deity he is invoking a trick of Vedic priestly poetry which has long been noticed as one of its most peculiar and characteristic features. When, however, Indra is said to have prepared the way for Surya, or, "caused him to shine", it is no more than good myth-rhetoric. For we can well imagine 'Word' from personal observation mana the sun-god so overwhelmed in battle with Ahi, Vritra, and other cloud-demons as to be unable to extricate himself and overcome his foes without the help of the Thunderer's weighty arm: in plain prose 'Word' a thunderstorm clears the sky and allows the sun to shine. It is, in substance, the same myth as that contained in a passage which tells how" the gods lifted Surya out of the sea [***samudra***] wherein he lay hidden" (X., 72). Not less transparent is the request to Indra that he should "hide the sun", here likened to a wheel, and direct his bolts against SHUSHNA, the Demon of Drought. But this short verse also very clearly shows how Surya, on certain occasions, could be regarded by Indra, on behalf of men and nature generally, as an enemy and a nuisance, to be suppressed, at least temporarily at all cost. For when battle is to be waged in earnest against the wickedest of all fiends, the blazing disc, or wheel, of the sun is hardly a desirable auxiliary. So that we do not wonder at the climax when Indra is praised for having, with the help of Soma, broken a wheel from Surya's chariot and sent it spinning downhill, thereby laming "the great wizard".[5]

This fine old Aryan custom endured far into the classical Brahmanic period, and the epics frequently show us noble maidens holding solemn levees on such occasions-the so-called *Svayamvaras*-a custom abundantly vouched for by the traditions of other nations of Aryan stock-Greeks, Teutons, Celts. In her father's house the Aryan maiden enjoyed the usual shelter and cherishing, and her brothers were her born champions and protectors. For we find passages in the rig-Veda where the fate of the brotherless orphan maiden is deplored because she has to look out for a husband herself, and those who wrong such a maiden are said to be "born for that fathomless place" the nameless pit of darkness into which Varuna casts evil doers. The sacredness of the marriage tie and the marriage rite in impressed on men in truly Vedic guise by a description a marriage in heaven, which forms the introduction to the wedding hymn. This marriage of Surya, the Sun maiden, with Soma, is evidently presented as the prototype of all earthly marriages, and as attesting the divine origin of the institution. That in this case, as always, their heaven was only a reflection of their earth, never occurred to the pious performers of the rite, for of *that* no people is ever conscious,-not the masses, anyhow. Surya is a daughter of Savitar, who gives her, "consenting in her heart", to Soma. The Ashvins are the bridegroom's best men (who made the demand), and Agni is the bride's escort (who rides before her and brings her to her husband). The naturalistic interpretation of the myth presents no great difficulty. The Sun-maiden (only another form of the dawn), can very well wed with soma in any of his capacities. Perhaps, though, his sacerdotal aspect, as king of sacrifice, is the most appropriate, not merely because of the Dawn's connection with holy rites, but chiefly because the development of the simple myth-nucleus shows Surya to have undergone the spiritually ritualistic transformation as so many originally naturalistic myth-persons, into an impersonation of Prayer. The enumeration of her bridal paraphernalia is wholly symbolic: "Beautiful in soothe were Surya's bridal robes.": they were made of different sacred metres. Heaven and earth were the frame of her chariot, that chariot itself "her heart's thought", hymns were the beams that supported it, "the two ears" the wheels, "knowledge" was her cushion, "seership" her jewellery; sacred songs were the diadem on her; brow and ornaments in her hair; the Rig and the *Saman* were the steers who draw her chariot "along the easy path of heaven". We have here all the pomp and circumstance of Vedic sacrifice, and the symbolical description ends with this remarkable verse: "Two wheels of thy chariot, O Surya, the Brahmans know, according to truth; but the third, the hidden one, is known only to the deep-inquiring". The allusion is here to "the two worlds", visible and known to all, and to that third world, mysterious, invisible, which is the very sanctuary where the origin of the things (of the gods) is forever hidden from mortal sight, and towards which the searching thought of the seers is ever drawn. Yet in the face of all this, the popular impression seems to have been that the marriage of Surya and Soma is that of the Sun (feminine, as in Germany) and the Moon.[6]

Notes and References

1. A.C. Clayton; *T.R.V.A.V.R;* p. 15.
2. *V.I.;* p. 275.
3. Romila Thapar; *A History of India;* Vol. I. First Published in 1966, 1990, 12th, 2002, New Delhi; p. 28
4. *V.I.;* pp. 215-216.
5. *Ibid;*., pp. 216-219.
6. *Ibid;*., pp. 368-370.

4

History of Vaishyas

The working class-*Vaishyas* (farmers, craftsman and traders[1]), *had to tend cattle, to bestow gifts, to offer sacrifices, to study the Veda, to trade, to lend money, and to cultivate land.*[2] In Vedic times the Vaishya, or mercantile class, though entitled to the services of the priesthood and to sacred thread of initiation, was but a poor third to the *brahmans* and *ksatriyas*. In the *Aitareya Brahaman* passage to which we have referred to *vaishya* is described as "paying tribute to another, to be lived on by another, to be oppressed at will". Other passages in early Brahmanic literature show him as a wretched and down-trodden cultivator or petty merchant, who is of no interest to his betters except as a source of profit. According to Manu the special duty of the *vaishya* was keeping cattle, which were made over to his charge at the creation of the world. The class evidently originated in the ordinary peasant tribesman of the *Rig-Veda,* but long before the law-book ascribed to Manu was composed it had many other activities. The *sudras,* the humblest of the four classes, had by now taken to agriculture, and admits many other legitimate *vaishya* occupations besides cattle rearing and farming. The ideal *vaishya* has expert knowledge of jewels, metals, cloth, threads, spices, perfumes and all manner of merchandise he is, in fact, the ancient Indian businessman. Though the Brahaman literature gives the *vaishya* few rights and humble status, the Buddhist and *Jaina* scriptures, a few centuries later in date and of more easterly provenance, show that he was not always oppressed in practice. They mention many wealthy merchants living in great luxury, and powerfully organized in guilds. Here the ideal *vaishya* is not the humble tax paying cattle-breeder, but the *asitikotivibhava* the man possessing with millions *panas*. Wealthy *vaishyas* were respected by kings and enjoyed their favour and confidence. It was they, rather than the kshatriyas, who chiefly favoured the rising unorthodox religions of Buddhism and Jainism. They formed by this time, at least in the regions of Magadha and Kosala, a true bourgeoisie, no doubt small in number, but very important. Numerous inscriptions from Sunga times onwards record the great donations of *vaishya* merchants and skilled craftsmen to religious causes, especially to Buddhism, and show that they were prosperous and influential. If the *vaishya,* according to *Aitareya Brahmana,* was to be oppressed at will, the lot of the *shudra* was even more unfortunate. He was "the servant of another, to be expelled at will, to be slain at will" but the latter phrase may be interpreted "to be beaten at will", and the import of whole passage seems to be satirical.[3]

Notes and References

1. V.I; P. 274.
2. *Ibid.*, p. 275.
3. A.L. Basham; *T.W.T.W.I.;* pp. 142-143.

5

History-Problem, Spirituality and Dr. Baba Saheb Ambedkar

Term History[1] has been composed of two English words that is 'His+story'. 'His' means *'God', 'Word', 'Shabd'* or *'Nad'* is undeciphered in Indus[2] scripts.[3] 'Story'[4] means 'history of world, which is untrue and destructive one. World had been put together by the 'Word', in Hindi it is called 'US-KI-KAHANI' means God and real living *man*. As early as the time of Lord Buddha,[5] world is the body of 'Word' made of five elements-earth, water, fire, air, and ether. All these five elements are antagonistic to one another. Earth is dissolved by water, water is dried by fire, fire is consumed by air, and air is absorbed by ether. But the soul in body gives life to these five elements and makes them compatible with one another. The movement the Lord withdraws the soul from the body, we die and earth merges in earth, water merges, in water, fire merges in fire, air in air, and ether in ether.[6] The soul gives life to everybody. He is everywhere, in everything, hence everything is God.[7] *In the beginning was the 'Word' and the 'Word' was with God, and the 'Word' was God (1:1).*[8] It is an orthodox theory of six fundamental *ragas* that is *Bhairava, Malkausika, Hindola, Dipaka, Sri-raga and Meghamachara. Each ragas has five raginis.* In some systems, their are also by bird called *putras* or sons, eight to each *raga. Ragas* are classified according to the time of the day or night for which they are most appropriate.[9] It is an 'Inner Voice' only those can hear, who has practiced the 'Word' or 'Nam'. 'Father' or God himself is a shining 'Light' within everyone of us, but we do not see that 'Light' now. When we close our eyes we see only darkness within. Why do we not see that 'Light'? Because in the process of creation, the soul, in its descent, became embedded and entangled with mind to such an extent that mind prevents the Light of soul from shining through. This is because, having come from the Father to the level of creation, the soul has forgotten the Creator. And the mind, being attached to the creation and its sensual pleasures that is eyes, ears, nose, mouth, two lowers hole organ of the body has collected a lot of sins, or Karmas, during many past lifetimes. These are called natural numbers in mathematics from 0 to 9 and every languages have been developed from them. This has clouded the mind to such an extent that it has become an impenetrable covering over the soul a veil of darkness, which prevents us from enjoying or seeing the Light.[10]

Everybody knows that *Shudras* formed the fourth *Varna of the Indo-Aryan* society.[11] At the time at which we begin to them *'Arya'* meant *'noble' 'exalted' 'venerable'* the name had become something almost sacred.[12] We called 'Aryas' primeval home an, "inland home", and later stated that "they had never be held the sea nor ocean". This is suggested by the fact that no name fore "sea " found in their earliest known language.[13] For everyone who has learned and taught knows what a weary long time the beginnings of any science or art take to master, and that, once the first principles are really and firmly grasped, the rest comes with a wonderful and ever-increasing rapidity, with a rush, as it were, partly owing to the training which the mind has undergone in the effort to step from "not thinking" to 'thinking' and partly because these same "first principles" really contain the whole art or science, which is only evolved from them, as the variations from the plot, or the plant from the seed.[14] Let us then try to open the intellectual treasure house of our earliest forebears with the golden keys they left for our use: their words. We may not yet enquire what they did with them; that they *had* them is their crowning glory and our gain; even greater than the wonders of literature in which they culminated. For, in the 'Words' of one of the greatest master of the 'Words, their histories and their uses, "our poets make poems out of words; but every-word if carefully examined, will turn out to be itself a poem, a record of a deed done or of a thought by those to whom we owe the whole of our intellectual inheritance..." Take, for instance, the word *PITAR-father,* the meaning of which is threefold-"feeder", "protector", "ruler": does not the underlying connection between these at the first glance different conceptions already warrant, by the subtlety and depth of observation which they betray, the same writer's enthusiastic assertion': "Wherever we analyze language in a scholar like spirit... we shall find in it the key to some of the deepest secrets of the human mind...." And does it not speak for an already highly developed moral feeling that the root PA, from which is formed *pitar,* the most generally used word for "father", does not *mean* " to give birth" but to protect, to support, showing how entirely the Aryan father realized and accepted the idea of duty and responsibility towards those who belonged to him by the most sacred of human ties. Each duty gives corresponding rights, just as each right imposes a duty, that the eternal fitness and balance of things may be maintained, that universal dualism, moral and physical, which is very root and sold of the world. And thus it is that it has been admitted from all time as self-evident that he who fulfils the duty of supporting and protecting a family, has the undisputed right of governing it, of imposing his will as the law of those who depend on his toil and affection for their sustenance, comfort, and safety. Hence *pati,* "master". This is, in few words, a complete definition of the word *"patriarch",* in which the Greeks, by a trick of language familiar to them, and, among the moderns, to the Germans, have deftly embodied the two indivisible conceptions: "father and ruler." *The word "patriarch"* occurs for the first time in the Septuagint, consequently came into use at a period much late than the golden age of Greek speech. Its immediate derivation or rather composition is from *patrid* or *patra,* "a clan, a tribe" and *arkheo,* "to rule", giving the meaning, "ruler of a clan or tribe", This, however, in no wise impairs the remoter, original association of ideas between *pater,* "father", and *patria',* "tribe",; in fact, it still more clearly establishes the twofold-domestic and political-character of word *patri,* "clan",-the family grown into the tribe, and the father of the one into the ruler of other. Another enlargement-and the tribe has become a people, a patriarch a king. This word *"pitar"* we can easily pursue through most Aryan languages, ancient and modern, although, as is the manner of the words in their wanderings, it now takes on a letter, now drops one, now alters a vowel or even some of its consonants, until it becomes barely recognizable to the trained eye and ear of the philologist. Thus Sanskrit *pitar* (Avestan *pitar* also), can hardly fail to be at once identified in *pater* (Greek and Latin), can easily be known in *vater* and *father,* the form derived by the two northern sister languages from the old teutonic *fadar;* the relationship is not quite as obvious in *padre* (Spanish and Italian), and especially in the French *pere;* indeed, the three southern Latin sister-tongues may be said to have adopted decided corruptions of the original word, and when we come to Celtic *athir, athar* (Gaelic, Welsh, Irish, Armorican), nothing short of scientific training will suffice to establish the identity. The word for "mother" is even more generally in use in the various Aryan languages, and has undergone fewer alterations. The Sanskrit *matar,* unchanged in *Avestan matar,* accept in accent, scarcely deviates in the Greek *meter* and Latin *mater,* which abides in the Slavic *mater,* only slightly shortened by modern Russian into *mati,* very recognizable for once in the Celtic *mathi,* even more than in the German *mutter,* and English *mother,* from Old Teutonic *muotar,* but corrupted in the Spanish and Italian *madre* and the French *mere,* after exactly the same fashion as the word for "father", evidently with conscious intention to establish a symmetry akin to alliteration-a rhyme a trick of language by which it pleased a slightly barbaric ear and taste to couple together kindred objects or ideas. The root of this multiform word is MA, "to make", and also "to measure". A combination particularly suggestive, since the mother, she who "has given birth", is also she who "measures", "portions out" the provisions, the food, and the other necessaries of life to the various members of the household. From the same root we have *mas,* the moon, the measurer of time, so that the same word means "moon" and "month", as it still does in its Slavic form, *"mesiats"*. The other words expressing near relationship are no less generally preserved in the several Aryan languages. To begin with: *Sanskrit bhratar-svasar; Avestan, bratar hvanhar, Greek, frater,* (only the word, at the stage of which it comes under our ken, had become diverted from its original meaning and was in a political or social sense, to designate a member of one of the tribes or the brotherhoods-*fratrias*-into which citizens were divided. For the family relationship of both brother and sister the Greeks adopted and entirely different word). Latin, *frater-soror;* Old Teutonic, *brothar-svistar; modern German, bruder-schwester, English brother-sister; Italian, fratc, fratcllo-suora, sorclla. (Fratc and suora* are used exclusively to designate religious brotherhood and sisterhood, "monk" "nun". *Frate* in this respect answers to the English *friar.)* Slavic and Russian, *brat-sestra;* Celtic, *brathir-suir,* French *frcre-soeur.* Take further Sanskrit, *duhitar,* Avestan, *dughdhar,* Greek, *thugater,* German, *tochter,* English *daughter;* Irish *dear;* Slavic, *dushter* (the pronunciation can not be understood from the written word, but must be heard and imitated); Russian, *dotcher, dotch;* Latin and her chief daughter languages, Italian, Spanish, and French, have adopted another designation, *filia-figlia-hija-fille.* The secondary family ties-those by marriage-are no less nicely determined-which in itself speaks highly for an advanced state of social order, and the words denoting them also turn up in most Aryan languages, some in many, others in but a few. One example must satisfy us; Sanskrit *devar,* "brother-in-law", is almost unchanged in the Russian *dever* and Lithunian *deveris,* and very recognizable in the Greek *daer* and even the Latin *levir.*[15]

We will conclude with a word embodying bereavement as universal as the family relations, and therefore reserved even more faithfully than many others through most languages of Aryan stock *vidhava,* "window", German *wittwe,* Russian *udova;* Latin, *vidua;* Italian, *vedova* corrupted by Spanish into *viuda* and by French into *veuve.* A word of mighty import, especially to later and modern India, as it mean "husbandless", and so would alone, suffice to prove that in enforcing the horrible practice of widow-burning or *sati-parikashan*[16] on the ground of sacred tradition, the Brahmans have been guilty of heinous misrepresentation; for, if the custom had, as they assert, existed from the beginning of the time, there would have been no *vidhavas,* no "husbandless women". Now they not only existed, but, we shall see later on, are repeatedly mentioned, and once in the religious service attending the burial (or, later, the burning) of the dead, explicitly addressed, as returning from the grave or the pyre to stay among the living. All this in the book which the stay among the living. All this in the book which the Brahmans regard as the holiest in all their sacred literature. Further more, in their law books, also invested with sacredness, windows are provided and legislated for at great length. So that the Brahmans stand convicted of deliberately falsifying, at least in this one instance, their own most sacred and, as they believe and assert, *revealed texts* (Figs. 11 and 12). And thus the English authorities, merely through ignorance of the natives literary language and their classic literature, were placed in the atrocious necessity of tolerating this abomination or breaking that portion of their agreement with the Hindus by which they engaged not to interfere with any of the religious observances. Now that the text themselves and their correct interpretation have been given to the world at large by the life long labours of our great Sanskritists, the government's hands were free to forbid and prevent, by armed force if necessary, these unnatural sacrifices. The abolition of the time honoured horrors of the widow burning or *sutte* the (more correctly written *sati*), yields us one more convincing proof of what tremendous practical issues may be waiting on the mere *study of words,* patiently, peacefully carried on by scholars in their quite studies and libraries, so remote in space and spirit from the battle-places of the work a day world.[17]

Now as regards intellectual achievements and abstract speculation, we must not be too prompt to desperate the efforts of our fathers on this ground on the plea that there is no common word for "thousand" in our languages,-or, more correctly in the parent languages of ours-Sanskrit, Greek, Latin, Old Teutonic having each fabricated a word of its own, which their respective offspring, dutifully adopted with the usual tribal alteration.[18]

One word to conclude this, on the whole, introductory chapter. We have come to speak quite familiarly of "the Aryas; primeval home", of their separations and migrations, as though we knew all about these subjects. We are, in a sense, justified in so speaking and imagining, on the testimony afforded by the formation and evolution of languages, of which we can, to a great extent, pursue the track over across the vast continent which, though geographically one, has been artificially divided, in conformity with political conditions and school conveniences more than with natural characteristics, into two separate parts of the world: Asia and Europe.[19]

It is sufficient to know that centre, no matter whence the primeval Aryas of all-the Proto-Aryas-may have come, has been a station on which a large portion of the race must have been sojourners for many centuries, that portion of it, at all events, of which the two principal limbs, the leading sister nations of the Aryan East, Eranians and Hindus,[20] divided almost within our ken, for reasons easy to conjecture, if not to establish with actual certainty, and some of which have been alluded to in former volume.[21]

Dr. Baba Saheb Ambedkar has rightly stated that the centre of religion lay not in the relation of man to God. It lays in the relation between man and man. The purpose of religion is to teach man how he should behave towards other men so that all may be live happy.[22]

Notes and References

1. It is a thousand pities that the Rig-Veda does not contain history in the direct narrative or epic form, but only in that indirect and fragmentary form which is known as "*internal evidence*". The reason is that the book represents not a simple and primitive state of culture, as has been, somewhat rashly, taken for granted for a number of years, but, on the contrary, an advanced and complex one, which had developed some essential social institutions, such as royalty, aristocracy, and priesthood, in clean-cut, strongly set frames, on the background of an already long and eventful national past. The consequences is that the hymns which we may designate as in a specially direct sense "historical" ones, are full of allusions to occurrences which everyone is supposed to know about, of names familiar to all. And where the occurrences and the names do belong exclusively to the world of Myth,[1] *based on Greek word 'mutho', traditional story concerning the early history of*

a people of explaining a natural or social fact and widely held but false belief, that also was too well and too generally understood to require explanation. Thus it comes to pass that the kernel of historical fact for which we seek is, to us latecomers, unaided as we are by any thinnest thread of memory or tradition, imbedded in an almost impenetrable thickness of hardest outer shells and prickliest burrs. Yet enough very essential facts have already been elicited by close and minute study, to form an interesting and on the whole unreliable general presentation of the Aryan advance from their first quarters in the Penjab eastward to that vast region watered by the historical fact for which we seek is, tous late-comers, unaided as we are by any thinnest thread of memory or tradition, imbedded in an almost impenetrable thickness of hardest outer shells and prickliest burrs. Yet enough very essential facts have already been elicited by close and minute study, to form an interesting and on the whole unreliable general presentation of the Aryan advance form an interesting and on the whole unreliable general presentation of the Aryan advance from their first quarters in the Penjab eastward to that vast region watered by the historical Ganges and Djumna, which became the centre and headquarters of the race when the Vedic era had glided by and merged into the Brahmanic period. Scant as we think the material which the Rig-Veda supplies for a reconstruction of an age too remote to be called epic, let alone historical, the results obtained are yet important enough to justify an epitome of them even in a popular work so necessarily limited in scope and space as the present. As few broad strokes of the brush will sketch an outline which will keep filling itself in with every added detail or scrap of "*internal evidence*", from the moment the point of view and the prospected are properly established, and it is these which will have to be shifted considerably from the originally accepted, long maintained lines, producing, on the whole, an entirely different picture, and one which, while it opens out a vista into a remoter past than was heretofore credited to our knowledge of India, presents some (if we may so express it) startlingly modern features; only another way of reasserting what has been found out by philosophizing students of our race so many ages ago as to have become a truism, namely that *"history repeats itself"*, and that "there is nothing new under the sun". Thirty-five years ago no one would have thought of connecting India (pre-Aryan India), with archaic Babylonia, and if a solitary fact pointing that way was once in a while picked out by an exceptionally inquisitive and observant mind, it was suffered to remain unexplained as a sort of natural curiosity, for the inferences it suggested were too startling to be more than hinted at.[2] (1. *V.I.;* p. 303. 2. Ibid. pp. 303-305). **Note:** Term *'History'* originated from Greek word 'historia' means the study of past event, considered as a whole connected with someone and something's and continuous recorded of the past events or trends called 'History'

2. **Note:** Term 'indus' is also composed of two words that is, In+dus, 'In' means 'within', 'dus' means 'absorb' in the body that is 'Name' or 'Word' according to the advise of the Perfect Master, who is present at Bias. Once you loose this human form, you will not get it again so easily. The Lord does not stay in these temples of bricks and mortar that we make for 'His' residence. 'He' is right within your body; but, says Christ, you do not bother to see 'Him' in your body. You worship the Father in these man made temples. You do not care for the temple that the Lord has given you and in which He resides. He calls the human body the temple of living God, because in this temple and in no other can we live wit God and become God. The Lord has given us this human form just for one purpose: to realize Him. If we misuse or destroy this temple by remaining attached to worldly treasures, we will not get this opportunity of the human form again so easily. (Maharaj Charan Singh; *Light On Saint John;* First

edition 1967; 2nd; 1971. 3rd 1974; 4th 1978. 5th 1985. 6th 1994. 7th 1996; Punjab (India), p. 33. Hereafter explained as *L.O.S.J.*)

3. Dr. V.K. Jain. *The Nature of Political Structure During The Harappan Period A Review;* An Article presented in the Punjab History Conference, March 18-20;2005; p. 1.

4. Word 'Story' has been originated from Old French word *'estorie'* means an account of imaginary or real people, and events told for entertainment an item of new, and informal a false story.

5. A.L. Basham; *T.W.T.W.I.*; p. 496. **Note:** Lord Buddha means Lord of the 'Wisdom' that is called 'Word' or 'Nam'.

6. Maharaj Charan Singh; *L.O.S.J.* pp. 11-12.

7. The *A's In-I-Akbari: By Abul-Fazl Allami,* Tr. by H. Blochamann; M.A. New Delhi; Vol. 1. 1989; p. 171. **Note:** Term Sufis' is made of two words i.e. Su + fis, 'Su' means 'love' and 'fis' means, a set of equipment for reproducing high fidelity of sound i.e. *(nad)* or *'Kalma'* or *'Word'*. Therefore everyone has to love with 'Him'.

8. Maharaj Charan Singh; *L.O.S.J.*; p. 9.

9. A.L. Basham, *T.W.T.W.I.* p. 383.

10. Maharaj Charan Singh; *L.O.S.J.*; p. 12.

11. Dr. Baba Saheb Ambedkar; *Who were the Shudras?* First edition 1946; 2nd edition *Independence Day*, 15th August; 2003; Aurangabad (India), p. 19.

12. *V.I.*, p. 62.

13. *Ibid.*, p. 72.

14. *Ibid.*, p. 74.

15. *Ibid.*, pp. 66-70.

16. Plate X (A) (Fig. 11) D.A.G. Jammu. Acc. No. 104/151 Sub : Sati Prakashan, School: Kangra. 18th century A.D.

    (B) (Fig. 12) D.A.G. Jammu. Acc. No. 105/152 Sub: Sati Prakashan, School : Jammu. 18th century A.D.

17. V.I., pp. 70-72.

18. *Ibid.*, p. 73.

19. *Ibid.*, p. 74.

20. **Note :** Term 'Hindus' which has been composed of four English words i.e. Hi+n+du+s. 'Hi' means having to do with high fidelity sound i.e. '*nad*'. 'N' stands for 'Nadir' means the lowest or worst point in Arabic, opposite to the zenith i.e., *man*, 'du' means 'two' soothed of two words i.e. d+u, 'd' stands for 'destruction' or 'untrue' i.e., *mana* or Brahmana and 'U' stands for 'unique', or 'wonderful' i.e. *'Nam'* or *'Kalma'* or *'Word'*. Any one can trade of 'Him' either Hindu or Sikh or Christian or Arabs. 'S' stands for ' sainthood', originated Old French Word 'saint', meaning 'of India'. 'of' is composed of two English alphabets o+f, 'o' stands for *'infinite'* and 'f' stands for *'false'* i.e. *man*. Term India' which has been put together of two words' In+dia: 'In' means within 'dia' means 'Light'. 'He' is right within the body, but we never bother to see 'Him' in the body. So far as the term 'Arabs' is concerned, it is composed of four words A+ra+b+s, 'A' stands for 'one' single in both the English and Hindi languages alphabets 'ra' means 'way', 'thought', 'b' stands for 'bliss' and 's' stands for 'sainthood', originated Old French word, 'saint'. Thus, the '*word*' is one, but *Brahmans* made unlimited.

21. V.I., p. 76.

22. Dr. Baba Saheb Ambedkar; *The Buddha and His Dhamma;* Nagpur (India); 1997; p. 254.

PLATE

Plate X

Fig. 11-Dogra Art Gallery Jammu; Acc. .No 104/151
Sub; ***Sati Prakashan;*** School-Kangara; 18th century A.D.

Fig. 12-Dogra Art Gallery Jammu; Acc. .No 105/152
Sub'; ***Sati Prakashan;*** School-Jammu; 18th century A.D.

Conclusion

From the above data, we learn that *Brahmans* or *manas* are criminals and they are committing rapes round the clock against the humanity. It is sufficient to prove that they are confronting with the Sanskrit language by misinterpreting the term '*Shudras*' means '*pure-thought*' which million years back has been lost in our thesis. Different Mystics, at different times, have referred to that some Power by different, names. Christ called it '*Word*', '*Logos*', '*Spirit*, '*Name*'. '*Holy Ghost*', and the '*Voice of God.*' Persian and Arabic Mystics have named it *Kalma, Bang-I-Asmani, Nada-I-Sultani, Ism-i-Azam, Sultan-AI-Azkar,* and many other names. Indian Mystics have called it *Akash Bani, Ram Nam, Ram Dhum, Nirmal Nad,* and, more generally, *Shabd,* or *Nam.* The Chinese called it *Tao.* This divine Power is also known by many other names.[1] Dr. Baba Saheb Ambedkar was an angel for all of us and was so kind that he has given an idea of the same called '*classless society*' or '*casteless society*' by providing the terms liberty, equality, fraternity and social justice in the Indian Constitution, even he has marked the ratio of the same race. The unity of Aryan speech is now established beyond the possibility of a doubt,[2] whose mode of life and state of culture we just now attempted to reconstruct. Reconstruct from what? From nothing 'the *Words*', which are the only heirloom they have transmitted to us, their late and widely scattered successors. Only '*Words*'. But as '*Words*' stand for thoughts, and knowledge, and feelings, this heirloom implies all our histories, all our philosophical system, our poetry in fact, all that we are and will be.[3]

Notes and References

1. Maharaj Charan Singh; *L.O.S.J.;* P. 5.
2. V.I.; p. 59.
3. *Ibid.*

Glossary

A

Aditi	Mother of Aditiyas
Aditiyas	Sons of Aditi
Agni	Fire, naturalistic description
Amrit	The drink of immortal from the nature
Ananta	Endless
Angiras	Nine natural numbers of the human body are called Angiras.
Antarala	For a long time.
Anu	Five tribes of the 'Word'.
Ariaka	The Aryan, snake god that is mana.
Aryas	Word, Nobel, Exalted, Pre-historic.
Arya Varta	Story of the 'Word'
Ashvins	The morning twilight
Asura	Originally the Aryan title of beneficent beings, later trans-

	ferred to evil beings, demons or fiends.
Atharva-Veda	The fourth Veda, incorporated late, different from the other three.
Atharvan	A mythical priest, who celebrate false belief.
Atharvans	A class of priest
Atmana	The self, the soul of the world
Atmosphere	The third world, ruled by Varuna
Avatar	(Incarnation of Vishnu), Third-Tortoise, Sixth Parashu Rama, first Fish (Matsya).

B

Battle of the Ten Kings	Ego and Infinite, 10.
Bias	Viyas, modern name of one of the 'Five Rivers'.
Bhagavata Purana	Old rivalry of the God and Mana
Bharatas	Story of the God or 'Word'
Bhrigus	Mana, 'finders'
Brahma	Prayer of the mana, in the form of sacred text.
Brahma	Suspense of the mind or mana
Brahamanspati or Brihaspati	'Lord of Prayer'.

Brahmana	Priest of the mana, who is wandering in the material life.
Brahma-varta	Story of the suspense.

C

Caste	Spanish and Portuguese word 'casta' means 'lineage or tribe'.
Cow	Belief of darkness.

D

Daevas	Demons, fiends of darkness.
Dahyu	'Dasyu'-mana, Dasa.
Devas	Gods, morning of the 'Word'.
Divodasa	Tribal hero of the Tritsu.
Djumna	Yamuna .
Dravidians	Earth and-serpent Brahmans.
Dyaus	'Dyaus the Father' after seeking the 'Word' becomes 'Word'.

E

Ekam	'The One'.

F

Festival of serpents	*Mana ka tamasa.*

G

Ganga	'Son of God'.
Garbhagrha	House of the Ego or mana.
Gayatri	Without 'Word' mana cannot satisfy .

Gods	Devas, 'Words'.
Grihya-Sutra	Brahamans domestic rule.
Grimm, Jacob	Philogical law discovered by him.
Guru	A spiritual instructor, successor of the ancient purohitas. Master of Vedas.

H

Himalaya	'His' house is inside.
History	Originated Greek word 'historia'.
Hydraotes	Greek name of the Jhelam.
Hypasis, Hypanis,	Greek names of Bias Vipasis.

I

Ida	Spiritual daughter of Manu, destructive one.
Indus	Absorve within the body that is 'Word'.
Iravati	Epic name of the Ravi.
Iroti	Ravi.
Ithiasas	Legendary poems.

J

Jhelum	Modern name of the one of the 'Five Rivers'.
Jyotisha	(Astronomy), One of the Vedangas.

K

Kavyas	A short epic poems.
Kashatriyas	To protect the people.
Kutsa	The Puru Purukutsa.
Kuvera	The God of the wealth.

M

Magic	Little used in the Rig-Veda.
Mahabharata	Great story of mana.
Mandalas	Division of mana, or estimate of manas.
Mandapa	Fiends of darkness.
Mantra	'Word' or 'Shabad'.
Manu, man	'The Human Race' of Brahmana.
Manushya	One of the names for 'Man'.
Manyus	'Wrath' deified abstraction.
Marriage	Sacredness of the souls take the shape of the marriage as an Example of the 'Word'.
Martya	'Mortal' name for 'man'.
Maruts	Storm-winds, there is a dispute with Indra.
Mitra	A God of light.
Mrityu	Death personified.
Myths	False belief originated Greek word 'Muthous'.

N

Nagas	Snakes-manas.
Narak	A 'hell-world'.
Naturalism	Principal characteristics of the Rig-Veda, 'Word'.

P

Panis	A mythical robber tribe, Sarama.
Pantchanada	Brings to the Indus the united waters of the "Five Rivers", Penjab where first portion of India settled by Aryas.
Pitris	Father, Pa.
Polytheism	Embodied in the Rig Veda.
Prajapati	Lord of creatures.
Pramantha	Churning sticks, Prishni, the cloud-cow, mother of the Maruts.
Prithive	Earth, the mother of the everybody.
Purohitas	Family and tribal priest and national bards.
Puru	One of the 'Five Tribe', usually allies of the Tritsu. Heads the confederacy of the Ten Kings that is 'Word'.
Puru-kutsa	(Kutsa the Puru) King of the Puru, Ally of the Tritsu, beaten on the Parushni.

Puru-kutsi	Daughter of Purukutsa, mother of Trasadasyu.
Pushan	A solar deity.

R

Rakshasas	The cannibal wizard demons of epic poetry.
Ravi or Iroti	Modern names of the 'Five Rivers' Parushi: Iravati.
Rig Veda	Principal of Naturalism i.e. 'Word'.
Rishis	True way to see the Word conduct with Perfect Master at Present.
Roots	Philological meaning of the 'Word'.

S

Samraj	'King of Kings', highest royal title.
Samudra	Sagar of Love i.e. 'Word'.
Sanskrit	Beginning of the studies and first results, 'Words' traced out Through the various Aryan languages.
Sarama	Trust on Myths, poetry of 'Word' and the Panis.
Saramya Dogs	Yama's messengers, children of Sarama.

Sayana	Author of the standard commentary of the Rig Veda or Preacher of the "Word'.
Serpent	Dravidian symbol Earth, Worship of material life.
Shesh or Sheshna	King of Serpent i.e., 'Word'. Dravidian snake god.
Shruti	Revealed sacred literature i.e. 'Word'.
Shudras	'Pure thought' or 'word'.
Shutudri or Shatadru	Vedic name of the Sutlej.
Suttee	"Widow-burning" no authority for, in the Rig-Veda. Brahmanical literature made Sati.

T

Tala	A 'Hell-World' in Rig-Veda.
Trasadasyu	Powerful king of the Puru, Grandson of PuruKutsa, friends of the Aryas.
Tritsu	'Word' has the thirst of love, their victory on the Purushni.

U

Upanishads	Philosophical treatise of the 'Word' which the Brahmans did.

V

Vach	Divinized Speech, the Voice of the Gods.

Vaishyas	The working class.
Varna	'Word', 'Nam', Shabd' or 'Holy Ghost'.
Vasishtha	A Rishi, bard of the Tritsu.
Vasudeva	A surname of Vishnu.
Vayu	Wind.
Vishnu	The 'Preserver' in the Brahmanic Triad, 'poisons story'.
Vishvakarman	"The Artificer of the Universe".
Vishvamitra	Friend of the whole world i.e., God.
Vishvarupa	"Omniform".
Vivasvat	The father of Yama and Husband of Saranyu.

W

'Words'	The only material for the reconstruction of early Aryan Life.
World	The hidden "navel of the universe".

Y

Yadu	The one of the 'Five Tribes'.
Yadur-Veda	The second Veda.
Yama	The king of the dead, parallel with the Eranian Yima.

Yami	Twin sister of Yama.
Yamuna	(Modern Djumna).

Z

Zadades	Greek name of the Satluj.
Zeus	Zeus-pater, Greek equivalent of Vedi Dyaush pitar.

Bibliography

Primary Sources

1. Plate. I-*'Murder in the Temple',* Crime, Politics, Greed; The sordid story behind the Shankara-charaya's arrest *'Outlook Magazine'* Nov. 29, 2004. (Fig. 1)

2. Plate II-Most Foul slain *'Ex-Math'* functionary A. Shankraraman, Right 'Jayendra Saraswati' with Vijay Saraswati's brother Ragu, '*Outlook* Magazine'; Nov. 29, 2004. (Fig. 2)

3. Plate III-The Sixth Avatar (or Vishnu Incarnate as Parashu-Rama. The Exterminator of the *Kshatriyas)'.* (Collection made from *Vedic India;* written by Zanaide-A-Ragozin, New Delhi 1961). (Fig. 3)

4. Plate IV-The Churning of the Amirta (Vishnu's Third Avatar or Incarnation the *'Kurma'* or Tortoise Avatar). *(V.I.)* (Fig. 4)

5. Plate. V-Reception of a Guru or Spiritual Instructor (V.I.). (Fig. 5)

6. Plate VI-The Matsya Avatar, or First Incarnation of Vishnu in the form of a Fish to recover the Sacred books. Lost During The Deluge (V.I.). (Fig. 6)

7. Plate. VII-OANNES...THE GOD EA (V.I.). (Fig. 7)

8. Plate. VIII-the Shatadru or Shatudri (Sutlej). (Fig. 8)

9. Plate IX-(A) Portrait Brahmans of Bengal (=Aryas). (Fig. 9)

   (B) Portrait of Low-Caste Bengalese

   (=Dasyu) (Fig. 10) (V.I.)

10. Plate. X-(A) Dogra Art Gallery Jammu;.

    Sub: *Sati Parikashan.*

    School-Kangra.

    18th century A.D. (Fig. 11)

    (B) Dogra Art Gallery Jammu.

    Sub: *Sati Parikashan.*

    School Jammu.

    18th century A.D. (Fig. 12)

Principal Works Consulted

11. *A History of India,* Volume One. Thapar Romila, New Delhi; 1966, 1990 12th Edition; 2002.

12. *Annihilation of Caste*, Ambedkar, Dr. Baba Saheb, Aurangabad (Indian); First Edition; 15th May 1936; 15th August 2003.

13. *Die to Live*, Maharaj Charna Singh; Punjab (India); 1979, 1980, 1983, 1988, 1992, 1995, 1999.

14. *Light on Saint John*, Maharaj Charan Singh Punjab (India); 1967, 1971, 1974, 1978, 1985, 1994, 1996.

15. *The A's-in-I-Akbari by Abul Fazl's Allami*, Tr. by H. Blochmann, M.A. Vol. 1, New Delhi, 1989.

16. *The Buddha and His Dhamma*, Ambedkar, Dr. Baba Saheb (Nagpur) India; 1997.

17. *The Nature of Political Structure During the Harappan Period-A Review*, V.K. Jain, An Article Presented in the Punjab History Conference (Patiala). March, 18-20th; 2005.

18. *The Rig-Veda and Vedic Religion*, A.C. Clayton, New Delhi, 1931, 1981.

19. *The Wonder That Was India*, A.L. Basham New Delhi; 1954,1963,1967,1981,1985, 2003.

20. *Vedic India*, Zanaide-A-Ragozin; New Delhi, 1961.

21. *Who Were The Sudras?*, Ambedkar, Dr. Baba Saheb, Aurangabad (India), 1946, 15th August 2003.

22. Compact Oxford Dictionary Thesaurus and Wordpower Guide, Dictionary Editor; Cather Soanes, Thesaurus Editor-Alan Spooner. Project Editor Sara Hawker; Oxford University Press in India 2004.

The Effect of Meditation

23. Maharaj Gurinder Singh; Spiritual Gems, A Perfect Master. Listening of Satsangs Concerning with Bias.

Index

C

D

E

F

G

H

I

J

T

V

W

Y